Living Valu

A practical guide to rooting your school in Christian values

Living Values

Edited by Shahne Vickery

Published by
Jumping Fish Ltd
Church House, College Green,
Gloucester GL1 2LY,
United Kingdom

Copyright © 2011 Jumping Fish Ltd

ISBN 978 0 9566257 2 4

Designed and produced by
Stella Edwards, Sugar Ink Creative, www.sugarinkcreative.com

First published in Great Britain in 2011.

A CIP catalogue record for this book is available from the British Library.

LIVING VALUES
A Practical Guide to Rooting your School in Christian Values

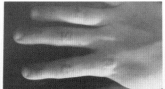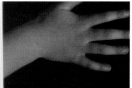

FOREWORD

In 2009 I was involved in a major review of the research that has been published on the impact of what we called "schools with a Christian ethos"[1]. This included Church of England Schools. What became apparent is that although many schools are excited by the prospect of offering a distinctively Christian education in their local community, a lot of them struggle to turn this aspiration into a reality. And there is a reason for that. Modern Britain is an increasingly complex place to be a Christian. We live in a richly diverse society when it comes to matters of religion whilst at the same time secular thinking is having a growing influence. Offering a distinctively Christian education that is appropriate for children that come from very different backgrounds is indeed a challenge.

Which is why Christian values are so important. Knowledge and understanding are obviously essential, but they are not enough for a Christian education. The influential report from the Children's Society, which painted a depressing picture of the experience of childhood in modern Britain, came to the conclusion that the pressure to succeed academically was of itself not helpful for children[2]. What they really need is to experience values that give them a sense of meaning and direction.

The influential positive psychology movement tells us the same; at root happiness is achieved through commitment to values, not financial advancement.

In 2004 I joined the Education Team at the Diocese of Gloucester and was introduced to Shahne's ideas on values. Prior to that I had extensive experience of publishing resources for schools and I immediately recognized that Shahne's work was something special. The long list of innovative publications at the end of this book bears witness to that. In this book Shahne offers another wonderful resource by drawing together the work of colleagues who, in their different ways, are making Christian values education a living reality. Reading through the chapters was a deeply encouraging experience. This cameo of professional wisdom means that teachers have access to support, advice and inspiration through reading the stories of colleagues. The aspiration to offer a distinctively Christian education can now be a reality for every school.

Trevor Cooling
Professor of Christian Education and Director of the
National Institute for Christian Education Research
Canterbury Christ Church University.

1 Green, Elizabeth and Cooling, Trevor (2009), *Mapping the Field: a review of the current research evidence on the impact of schools with a Christian ethos.* London: Theos
2 Layard, Richard and Dunn, Judy (2009), *A Good Childhood: Searching for Values in a Competitive Age,* London: Penguin Books.

INTRODUCTION

It has been said that there is no such thing as a values vacuum.

In every organisation, be it a golf club, care home or corner shop, a set of values will be operating. Whether or not those values are explicitly expressed in a mission statement or branding slogan, they will nonetheless be recognised in the way decisions are made and individuals are treated.

In recent years 'values' have also become big business. Multi-national corporations invest vast sums in the services of public relations professionals, who select for them the values that will best grow their companies. It is now widely accepted that ethos and values impact significantly on operational effectiveness and profitability.

Some years ago, whilst Minister for Education, David Blunkett was quoted as saying, *"I don't know what it is about Church schools, but I wish I could bottle it."* The leaders of Church schools however are able to identify very clearly what makes their schools distinctive, and one of the first factors that they will point to is their Christian values.

In the post-modern age, where individualism reigns supreme, a predetermined set of values will be considered by some to be unacceptably prescriptive and dogmatic. Nevertheless, rather than arbitrarily selecting a set of values that happen to sit comfortably with the prevailing culture, the Church school will instead look to the Bible as its source of inspiration, and especially to the life and teachings of Jesus Christ. Whilst many of these Christian values will be shared by those in society of no particular religious faith, others do not sit so comfortably in a secular context. For example, the Christian understanding of the value forgiveness will be rooted in the nature of God himself.
"The Lord our God is merciful and forgiving." (Daniel: 9.9)

The supreme demonstration of forgiveness for the Christian is seen in what Jesus accomplished on the cross. St. Paul writes:
"Be kind and compassionate to one another, forgiving each other, just as in Christ, God forgave you."
(Ephesians: 4.32)

Local clergy and church school leaders are actively engaged in a reflective consideration of Christian values and their place in education. One vicar commented: *"Shining the light of our Christian values on the thorny issues that we governors need to grapple with, such as capability procedures, staff appointments and policy development, has led to some real soul searching for all of us."*

Such has been the impact of values lived out with integrity in the school context that headteacher Helen Springett, writes of her former school, *"Once embedded into school life Christian values, or Gospel values as we called them, became so intrinsic to everything that we did, that nothing else was required in terms of our behaviour code. In our school our values were clearly understood by the whole community, from four year olds to adults, pupils to parents. Where behaviour fell below expectations, our children were encouraged to review their behaviour against these values."*

It is now over five years since Jumping Fish published *Values For Life*, a resource for collective worship based on the values justice, forgiveness, peace, friendship, courage, creativity, generosity, service, wisdom, compassion, trust, respect and reverence, humility, truth, thankfulness, hope, perseverance and responsibility. The popularity of this publication continues to generate other Jumping Fish material which supports values education and spiritual development. Together the titles have become known as *The Values Toolkit*.

The purpose of *Living Values*, the latest addition to this toolkit is, in the words of children, school leaders and teachers, to tell the stories of how values have become the starting point for policy making and educational practice in all aspects of school life. They describe what it is to live out Christian values in the classroom, staffroom and playground as well as on the PTA, the school council and in meetings of the governing body. These stories offer an intriguing insight into the revolution that is quietly unfolding in our schools and I am incredibly grateful to everyone who has shared their experiences so passionately as part of the *Living Values* project.

VALUES: VISION AND ETHOS

Margaret James is part of the Senior Management Team at St. Mary's Voluntary Aided Church of England Primary School in Thornbury, South Gloucestershire. She is a practising SIAS Inspector and also works part time as an RE Advisory Teacher for South Gloucestershire Local Authority. Margaret co-ordinates RE and Collective Worship in her school and is also a member of the Governing Body. In this chapter she describes how she led the process to re-engage her school community with values education, by asking which of the Christian values should stand at the centre of its life and work and how they would inform its developing vision and ethos.

The values would need to be explored in depth by the whole school community to be understood and relevant to everyday life.

Christian values have been an important part of our collective worship themes at St. Mary's for several years. However, a significant staff turnover resulted in many of our current teachers being unsure about how the values related to other areas of school life. Values seemed to have become an 'add-on' rather than principles informing our vision and aims and underpinning how we live together as a community. We felt that one of the reasons for this was that there were too many values for the children to remember and engage with.

In order for us all to truly own the Christian values of the school, the Senior Management Team (SMT) decided to embark on a concentrated period of consultation. We decided that a number of elements would be important to include in this process:

- The views of all members of the school community needed to be sought and considered.

- Whichever Christian values became our core values they needed to *underpin* the life of the

school rather than merely be trickled down through times of collective worship.

- The values needed to be explored in depth, in a variety of creative and inspirational ways, by the whole school community in order to be understood and relevant to everyday life.

We came up with the idea of holding a Vision Week!

Day 1

The Vision Week was launched on a sunny day in May at an outdoor Eucharist service held on the school field. Parents, governors, our Bishop's Visitor, diocesan officers and members of St. Mary's Parish Church who are involved with the life of the school were invited to attend. At this service, we prayed for God's blessing and guidance on the week ahead.

After the service, a number of boards were placed around the field and everyone was invited to write down their ideas about the values which they thought were already at the heart of our school and those they considered to be important which were currently not included.

Different activities were designed to draw out what children and adults really meant by the words they had used to describe their chosen values.

The questions asked were: "Which Christian values do you think are important for us at St. Mary's?" and "Which words or phrases describe something of your vision for our school?".

The brief list below gives a flavour of the feedback received:

Values	Our vision for the school
Unity	building confidence
Honesty	sharing life together
Justice	honesty in all our dealings
Respect	enriching the curriculum
Happiness	emotionally healthy
Tolerance	aware of people who think differently
Friendship	loyalty to one another
Humility	thinking of others before yourself
Kindness	politeness, care and thoughtfulness
Creativity	a culture to encourage exploration and wonder
Curiosity	

Day 2

The children were asked to think about what makes a value *Christian* and which values were absolutely central to the Christian faith. We looked together at some of Jesus' teaching from the Gospels and some key Old Testament stories and tried to suggest which values were emerging from these texts. All opinions were taken on board as long as the children were able to explain reasons for their ideas.

Day 3

The third day of Vision Week saw different activities for children, parents and governors, all of which were designed to draw out what children and adults really meant by the words they had used to describe the values.

The children took part in a glass painting workshop in which they discussed why each value was important to them. They painted representations of their values onto glass containers. The containers were designed to have a candle burning inside, symbolising the light of Christ shining through our lives when we live out the value.

Children, parents and governors talked about which values should be the starting point for our new behaviour policy.

A member of the Governing Body, who works as a behaviour support teacher, invited parents and governors to a discussion workshop on the review of the school's Behaviour Policy. Instead of our vision and values being added on at the end of the process, they talked about which values should be the starting point for our new policy. The views of those who attended were collated and incorporated into the final Behaviour Policy.

Day 4

Parents were given a day off but the pupils continued to make their suggestions about what they thought the vision and values of the school should be. Classes discussed the rights and responsibilities of each individual member of the school. The idea was to enable the children to develop their understanding of the place of each person in the school community and how their own behaviour has an impact on others.

Class teachers were encouraged to draw out of the discussions the idea that if our Christian values underpin how we behave and think about others, then we will naturally be focusing on our responsibilities rather than our rights and when everyone in the community does this, there will be no need to fight for our rights as everybody else is in fact already doing that for us.

The examples that the children gave of how values would impact on behaviour reflected minutiae of daily life in school and issues such as *"I shouldn't make fun of anyone else's work"* and *"we should let others join in our games at playtime"* were explored.

Suggestions made by the children in these discussions informed the writing of the School Charter and Rights and Responsibilities documents.

It is difficult to argue against upholding the schools values when you have had such a significant role in deciding what they should be!

Day 5

St. Mary's School has a Parents' Forum which meets 6 times a year. This group is open to all parents and governors and was used as a consultation body during Vision Week. The feedback from this meeting proved invaluable. The purpose and value of genuine consultation was plainly evident as parents explored their differing understanding of concepts such as "justice" and "freedom" and the impact these would have if they underpinned our practice. Differences of opinion were accepted and compromises were made. In a discussion about whether all the Fruit of the Spirit should be included, the Bible was consulted and the merit of each fruit was pondered.

For those 'professionals' concerned about any loss of control emanating from consultation with stakeholders – take note! The sense of worth felt and expressed by those who chose to be involved in this process has had long lasting benefits for the whole school community and has resulted in deeply felt ownership of the school's values and vision. It is difficult to argue against upholding the school values when you have played such a significant role in deciding what they should be.

Day 6

Having come to the end of the consultation process, it was time to make the decision about which 12 values would make the final cut! We had already sought the opinions of pupils, parents, members of the church, staff and governors so it was decided that the group making the final decision should be relatively small. Therefore, a governor, a teacher, the Head and I sat down with all of the suggestions and began to choose. Lengthy discussions ensued and the "chosen 12" came forth as follows: respect, forgiveness, perseverance, self-esteem, trust, honesty, love, co-operation, courage, joy, kindness and self-control.

No doubt, a different set of people within our school would have chosen different values but a decision had to be made!

Each class had the task of making a metre high, fabric banner to represent their understanding of the different aspects of their chosen value.

The new school values were announced to all of the pupils. Each class then chose a value which they specifically wanted to represent through the arts. For the rest of that day, the children worked on their class' value finding ways of exploring it through the media of art, dance, drama and music. The outcome of this time was shared with the whole school community at a special time of worship at the end of the week.

Day 7

To draw Vision Week to a close, on Day 7 the school descended into banner-making chaos. Each class had the task of making a metre high, fabric banner to represent their understanding of the different aspects of their chosen value. The banners displayed tangible interpretations of the values which the children could relate to. For example, the Year 6 class designed fabric squares each illustrating gifts and accomplishments that have boosted their self-esteem. The Year 3 group was inspired by the story of Daniel[1] when *Courage* was the value in focus.

They depicted Daniel praying for deliverance as the lion prowled around. The finished products are eye-catching and bring real colour to our acts of worship. They are processed into the school each Monday morning at the beginning of worship and then hung around the hall.

The children of St. Mary's are now entirely familiar with the school values and vision – they can certainly name each one and more importantly they can relate them to the way that they behave towards others and to the whole life of our community. At the start of meetings with parents and governors there is a reminder of our school values, establishing parameters for all discussions. The Home/School Agreement has been rewritten using the language of the school vision and values and as a result all parents, children and teachers are invited to reaffirm their commitment as they sign the agreement at the beginning of each school year.

1 Daniel 6.1-24

Visual and expressive arts are frequently used to draw out the emotional impact of the stories.

For many Church schools, including our own, there has been a lively debate about whether or not to use the Social and Emotional Aspects of Learning (SEAL) resource, which has an individualistic and, some feel, egocentric approach. Eventually we decided that SEAL should still play a part in the children's learning but that it's themes needed to fit in with and be driven by our Christian values and spirituality rather than the other way around. We want our emphasis at St. Mary's to be on the fact that God wants us to reach our full potential and use all our gifts, not because we will be more successful or popular individuals but because we are called to use these gifts and abilities for the good of our *whole* community and even the wider world. We therefore compiled a planning matrix for collective worship which clearly set out how the SEAL themes fit in with our values. In order to help the children to understand the values in the context of the Christian faith, we chose some key Bible stories which seem to us to exemplify where our values come from.

The stories are covered in depth in the following ways so that when children leave our school they are really familiar with them:

- The worship team dramatise the story drawing out the message and how it relates to the value;

- A Reflection Book offers children the opportunity to express their response to an aspect of the story;

- Key verses form part of the mini-reflection stations around the school;

- Children are encouraged to learn the verses;

- Children interpret the story through music including rapping, chanting and clapping;

- Visual and expressive arts are frequently used to draw out the emotional impact of the stories.

- We sing songs in worship which we tell the Bible stories in child friendly and fun ways. For example the wise man uilt his house upon the rock, songs from Joseph and his Amazing Technicolour Dreamcoat.

VALUES AND VISION MATRIX (for a 2 year rolling programme)

TERM	VALUE	VISION	BIBLE STORY	S.E.A.L THEME
1a	Respect	We all matter	Creation story (Genesis 1)	New beginnings
2a	Forgiveness	We learn from everything	The conversion of Saul (Acts 9.1-19)	Getting on and falling out
3a	Perseverance	We try our hardest	Call of Samuel (1 Samuel 3) Moses and the escape from Egypt (Exodus 7-14)	Going for goals
4a	Self-esteem	We try to keep healthy, inside and out	Joseph (Genesis 37 – 45) Jesus as a boy speaking with the Rabbis (Luke 2.41-52)	Good to be me
5a	Trust	We help each other to be safe	David & Jonathan (1 Samuel 19-20) Jesus calms the storm (Matthew 8.23-27)	Relationships
6a	Honesty	We are responsible for one another as well as for ourselves	Peter's denial of Jesus (Matthew 26.69-75) Peter in prison/ earthquake (Acts 16.23-34)	Changes

TERM	VALUE	VISION	BIBLE STORY	S.E.A.L THEME
1b	Love	We all matter	Noah's Ark (Genesis 5.9 - 9.17)	New beginnings
2b	Co-operation	We help each other to be safe	Rebuilding the city walls (Nehemiah)	Getting on and falling out
3b	Courage	We try our hardest	Shadrach, Meshach and Abednego (Daniel 3) Daniel in the lion's den (Daniel 6.1-23)	Going for goals
4b	Joy	We learn from everything	Prodigal Son (Luke 15.11-32) Song of Mary (Luke 1.46-55)	Good to be me
5b	Kindness	We try to keep healthy, inside and out	Ruth, Naomi and Boaz (Ruth) Jesus heals a man (Mark 2.1-12)	Relationships
6b	Self-control	We are responsible for one another as well as for ourselves	Temptation of Jesus (Matthew 4.1-11)	Changes

The parents decided that they would like to make large scale creative representations of the values.

Deciding together which Christian values define our school community has brought a sense of cohesion, unity and direction which did not exist before. Governors and parents involvement in sharing the values continues to go from strength to strength. At the beginning of the last school year, the Parents' Forum decided that it would like to make large scale, creative representations of the values, which could then be displayed in the school grounds and public spaces and encourage all parents to become as familiar with the values as the children already are.

The parents began this project with a photo shoot of "body-sized" letters. These were then used to spell out the values in a large photographic montage. The bodies used to make the letters were the parents themselves. Approximately 25 brave and resilient people gathered on possibly the coldest day of the year to lie out on a patch of grass in the Castle Hotel in Thornbury whilst local photographer, Chris Milne, captured them as the alphabet. The result will be a montage of all 12 values for the school reception area and the word "co-operation" writ large and displayed in the Hall.

Parents are also busy growing and propagating flowers which will be planted in the school playground to spell out "Love". They are planning to bring together the whole school community at a street party to share in the planting.

A Key Stage 2 musical composition group has been commissioned to write a school song which will be humorous and fun, but also help the children to remember the names of the values.

More than just resulting in a shared set of Christian values, St. Mary's Vision Week has established a community which is moving forwards and working together with a common aim and purpose. The school ethos is now firmly rooted in Christian values and we work hard to uphold them in all areas of the life of our school.

VALUES:
THE GOVERNING BODY

Neville Norcross is a former headteacher of a number of primary schools and is now a national trainer of SIAS inspectors. He also works with governing bodies throughout the UK to support, facilitate and explore their role as evaluators of their school's Christian distinctiveness. In this chapter Neville outlines a range of practical strategies to support the challenging but vital work of the Church School governing body.

The values of a church school are increasingly counter to the prevailing culture of our time.

Respond to your calling

Does God call the qualified or qualify the called? Most governors when taking up this important position feel ill-equipped for the challenges that lie ahead. This chapter explores a number of principles which, I hope, will go some way to supporting both new and experienced governors in the vital work they are called to do.

At the start of the new millennium the General Synod of the Church of England declared that "Church schools stand at the centre of the Church's mission to the nation."[1] Whilst the primary concern of church schools is not to evangelise, they *do* provide an excellent opportunity for the church to serve the children and families of the whole parish.

In his book *Supporting Christians in Education*[2] Professor Trevor Cooling refers to Daniel as a good role model. This Old Testament hero exercised counter-cultural leadership and overcame significant challenges in responding to his calling. Ultimately he became a successful leader who shaped the future

of his community. The values of a church school are increasingly counter-cultural to the prevailing values of our time. Our schools require enthusiasts rather than experts as governors who will support them in the challenges that they face.

Follow the guidelines

The legal framework, within which governors operate, gives them responsibility for the values, vision and aims which determine this school's direction of travel. An established set of values will provide a clear context for this journey. In one school the values were summed up in the passage from Jeremiah: "I know the plans I have for you, plans for a hope and future."[3]

This strap line, based on the value of hope, is the driving force behind all the decisions made within the school.

1 The Way Ahead Dearing Report 2001, Church House Publishing

2 Supporting Christains in Education, Trevor Cooling, pub. 2008 LICC

3 Jeremiah 29.11

There is a strong case to be made for having a governors' committee that ensures the strategic direction of the school is based on Christian values

Governors may wish to visit their school's Mission Statement and Aims and ask how far they reflect it's Christian character. The vision statement adopted by one school "Working Together. Aiming High." may roll nicely off the tongue but does not express the distinctive aims of a church school. However, the statement of another school, "Learning, Living and Loving in our Christian Community" explicitly describes the Christian context in which the education in that school will take place.

Strong evidence supports the view that a distinctive ethos based on Christian values is the best foundation for success. Primary league tables consistently show that whilst faith schools represent about one third of all schools in England, two thirds of the best-performing schools are faith schools.[1]

When we think of the welfare of pupils it is easy to be pre-occupied by issues such as safeguarding, site safety and anti-bullying policies. However, the church school governor should think also of welfare in terms of providing an alternative model of success to that

espoused by the media and often dominated by the values of consumerism, individualism and celebrity. We should ensure that children leave our schools having understood and experienced a set of values based on the life and teachings of Jesus. In short, we are called to be counter-cultural.

There is a strong case to be made for having a governors' committee which ensures that the strategic direction of the school is based upon Christian values and that these underpin the whole life of the school community. In some schools this body is known as the Ethos Committee and in others the Vision and Values Committee. It usually comprises the parish priest, foundation governors and headteacher. In Christ Church Infant School in Downend, Bristol the Ethos Committee uses the toolkit produced by the National Society to focus on developing a different aspect of the school's Christian foundation each year. This committee has been the main driver for improvement in the development of this successful church school.

1 Department for Education league tables 2010

Vision and Values Committee: Terms of Reference

The Terms of Reference for a Vision and Values committee might look something like this:

Membership

- The committee shall consist of up to 6 members of the Governing Body including the Headteacher who is an ex-officio member.

- Non-voting participants may be invited to meetings by the committee as and when required.

Quorum

The quorum shall be 3 members, including the Headteacher but excluding any co-opted non-voting members.

Meetings

The clerk to the committee shall be responsible for convening meetings of the committee. Procedures of any meetings must be minuted and these minutes presented for the next meeting of the Governing Body.

The committee will meet at least once a term and otherwise as required.

Responsibilities

The main function of the committee is to support, advise and challenge the Headteacher and the Governing Body on matters relating to the distinctiveness and effectiveness of ……………………………. School as a church school and the impact which this has on the pupils and whole school community, in particular:

a) the relationship between the school and …………………………… church

b) the development of joint projects between school and church such as a shared charity

c) the relationship between the school and the local, national and global communities

d) the impact of worship on the school community

e) the effectiveness of religious education

f) the impact of Christian values within the curriculum and the wider life of the school particularly in pupils' spiritual, moral, social and cultural development

g) the way in which the school makes provision for the future leadership of church schools

h) the way in which the Christian character of the school is monitored and evaluated in terms of its impact on pupils, staff, parents and the wider community

i) to make recommendations to the Governing Body on relevant policy matters

j) preparation for the Statutory Inspection of Anglican Schools

St. Michael's High School, Crosby

At St. Michael's High School in Crosby the PE teacher felt strongly that the curriculum in her department should reflect more explicitly the school's values. Among other things this led to values being thematically interpreted through dance and gymnastics, as well as a reorganisation of Sports' Day to strengthen a focus on sportsmanlike behaviour. The impact of the work was recognised by the school's Senior Leadership Team and the head of department was asked to lead a staff meeting to share the good practice. As a result, other departments were challenged to explore the school's values:

- The art department took pupils to look at Anthony Gormley's Iron Man in the Mersey Estuary. They then created their own iron man. After reading Ephesians Chapter 5 the students dressed him with *the belt of truth, the breastplate of righteousness* and *the shield of faith, (see above)* thus linking their work to the school's values.

- Office staff redesigned the entrance area and foyer to reflect the school's values through the displays, artefacts and notices.

- The music department produced a video on St. Michael's "Living Values" which was sent to the feeder primary schools.

- The school radio station produced a *Thought for the day* with pop-up values.

- A *Hope Board* was introduced and students were invited to contribute their hopes and dreams for the future.

- Banners were made and displayed around school to promote the school's values eg. *Have you shown compassion today?* and *Show respect, earn respect.*

St. Michael's was formerly a Community High School which was in danger of closing due to poor results and a falling role. The school is now thriving both academically and in terms of its outstanding ethos.

A church school is more than a school with religious bits tacked on to the curriculum.

Learn from others

The Christian Values for Schools website, www.christianvalues4schools.co.uk, developed by the National Society, was designed to provide practical support for schools, including governors, as they try to ensure that Christian values are an integral part of their work with young people. The site introduces 15 values from which schools can choose those which are the most appropriate for them. An introduction by the Archbishop of Canterbury reminds us that what is important about church schools is more than having "religious bits tacked on to the curriculum". The Christian ethos can have an impact on every aspect of school life.

Each value is accompanied by a theological background which enables us to have an accurate understanding of the Christian view of that particular value and its roots in the Bible.

The question has been asked "Why call these values *Christian* values?" The reason is that whilst a community school can legitimately select a set of values tailored to suit their own purpose, a church school will draw on the values running through the sacred stories of the Old Testament and the teachings of Jesus Christ. Convenient though it might be to omit uncomfortable values, such as forgiveness and humility, these are at the heart of the Christian gospel and are known as Kingdom values.

A recent addition to the National Society site has been the Values Blog, a means by which good practice can be shared. The site provides very helpful materials to support training activities and the all important church school self-evaluation.

This short piece cannot possibly do justice to the wealth of material which can be found on the site. It has been used extensively to challenge, support and encourage the many schools which are now looking to develop a programme of Christian values.

A training evening for Governors on Christian values

It is important that schools have a training programme for governors in addition to one for the staff. The programme should reflect the school's priorities as a church school. Set out below is a suggested outline.

1. Family Values – *5 minutes*
Introduce the idea of family values and ask the governors to write down some words that come into mind when they hear this phrase. Share their ideas and write on a flip chart.

2. Who do you admire? – *5 minutes*
Ask the governors to think about a famous person for whom they have admiration and write down the characteristics they admire in that person. Again share thoughts and record on the flip chart.

3. What is important? – *5 minutes*
Discuss: "People are usually valued for their personal qualities rather than their physical characteristics or intelligence."

4. The case for Christian values – *15 minutes*
In this session you will be highlighting the need for Christian values in our schools.

a) David Blunkett once famously said, "I don't know what it is about church schools but I wish I could bottle it". He recognized that something about the ethos, the values and the character of a church school provides the right foundation for academic and personal achievement. Discuss.

b) Engage the governors in discussion about:
  - changing family values
  - the impact of consumerism on young people
  - the impact of celebrity culture - famous for being famous

  For example; the media have recently reported that some secondary schools have now dropped non-uniform day because of the fact that those students who could not afford the designer clothes could feel embarrassed and often stay away from school. Is this acceptable?

5. If you don't stand for something you'll fall for anything" – *5 minutes*
We are called to be counter cultural. Refer to Psalm 137.4 "How do we sing the truth in a strange land?" and discuss how far the prevailing culture is/is not at odds with family values.

6. Fulfilling our responsibilities – *5 mins*
Church schools are places where the faith is lived and which, therefore, offer opportunities to pupils and their families to explore the truths of Christian faith, to develop spiritually and morally and to have a basis for choice about Christian commitment.[1]
Allow the governors to respond to this.

7. Mind Mapping – *15 minutes*
A technique to help governors understand how values can be found within a Bible story. Take a story of your choice, eg. the Widow's Mite from Mark 12.41-44. Put the story title in the centre of a large sheet of paper and ask the governors to identify all the values which they can find in this story and write them in the boxes around the outside. Some ideas are:
  - Generosity shown by the widow
  - Trust shown by the widow
  - Boastfulness shown by the rich – Humility
  - Sacrifice – shown by the widow

8. Learning from others – *20 minutes*
Choose examples from this book which illustrate values in displays and through aspects of school life. Focus on the way in which they make a difference to school ethos, pupil behaviour and attitudes and to personal and academic development.

9. Decide on the next step – An Action Plan – *20 minutes*
  ● Involve children, staff and parents in a consultation about the school values
  ● Audit where the values are working already and discuss the difference they are making
  ● Ask the children for their views on what particular values mean to them
  ● Launch your values at the start of a term with a *big event*
  ● Inform parents about your values through newsletters and other means
  ● Consider linking your School Mission Statement to the core values
  ● Ensure that values form an important part of your planning for daily worship
  ● Consider having a value of the month or term
  ● Discover ways in which values can be embedded in every aspect of school life – the curriculum; behaviour policy; sex & relationship education; PE; break times; etc.
  ● Look at the displays around your school and ask yourself if they make your values clear
  ● Review governors questions on the Christian Values for Schools website.

1 Quote is from The Way Ahead – Dearing Report

At St. Mary's Thornbury the values were velcroed in a diamond formation and parents were invited to rearrange the hierarchy giving their reasons.

Know your school

Governors of church schools are tasked to ask the right questions about the impact of Christian values in their schools. This is part of their evaluating and monitoring role. To undertake this role successfully they need the right information. Listed below are a number of straightforward and creative ways to get to know your school even better:

- The Learning Walk. A small group of governors, accompanied by a pupil or a member of the senior management team (SMT), walk around the school noting examples of Christian values in the displays. Conversing with the children (or SMT) the governors begin to understand the impact values are having on the lives of individuals.

- Photographs of the Learning Walk can be shown to other governors through a PowerPoint© display. The headteacher can explain the significance of each photo and how it demonstrates the impact of a particular value.

- Download the Values questions from www.christianvalues4schools.co.uk relating to one value each term. Use the open-ended questions to challenge the school with regards to the impact of that value within its daily life.

- Invite parents into school to engage in discussion about the values. At St. Mary's Thornbury the values were velcroed in a diamond formation and parents were invited to rearrange the hierarchy giving their reasons.

- Have the governors produce their own mind map showing how they believe a particular value might/does look in their school. Alternatively arrange for a governor to work with a group of children as they produce a mind map.

- A governor could join the School Council once a term to hear from them the impact of the value in focus.

VALUES: BUILDING YOUR STAFF TEAM

In this chapter Margaret James describes how the Senior Management Team (SMT) at St. Mary's Voluntary Aided Primary School in Thornbury, Bristol has recently reviewed their appointment process to take account of the school's work on values. They have found that explicitly referring to their values at each stage in the process has made a huge contribution to attracting the right people and making the right appointments.

I remember a display of 'friendship spoons' in the entrance, which embodied the emphasis on love and the value of each individual.

As all school leaders know, the process of selecting and appointing new staff is key to creating and maintaining a cohesive and successful team.
At St. Mary's we have discovered the hard way that to ignore the character of our school and our direction of travel in relation to our Christian values, when making appointments, is to leave out of the process the most important indicator of who we are as a community. This then leaves candidates unclear about what we are looking for in a prospective team member. Time and again we have found that simply following the job and person specifications in relation to the teaching commitment has led to a dead end, signposting us towards candidates whom we knew to be unsuitable in some way.

Having recently undergone the really illuminating process of identifying precisely what our school's core values should be *(see Chapter One: Values: Vision and Ethos)* we realised that we were looking for personnel who would be charged with upholding these values and inspiring others to live them out, without at any point asking candidates about their own personal values or whether they felt comfortable about our school values. It was not a giant leap of logic to conclude that we needed a root and branch review of our appointment process!

We considered each part of our procedure carefully and set about making some changes. As well as describing the professional requirements for the vacant post, our job adverts now make reference to our values and ethos, pointing candidates to find out more from our school website.

Likewise the person specification now clearly states that the successful candidate will be able to demonstrate how their own values, passions and personal qualities will contribute to the life of our school community. A letter of application that responds to this key element in the person specification makes the process of short listing so much more focussed when trying to decide between dozens of forms from teachers who are all similar in their professional suitability for the job.

We often ask focused questions such as "Is there a value that we have not included in our list that is especially important to you?"

When the interview day arrives, all candidates are first tasked with teaching a lesson to a class of children of a similar age group to that of the advertised post. Often we ask candidates to choose a text for a literacy lesson which has a value at the heart of the story and to explore this with the children as part of the lesson. Later in the day children are consulted about each candidate's quality of teaching, making reference to the pace, level of challenge and suitability of resources. They are also asked about the quality of relationship that the candidate was able to establish with the class. Our children recognise the importance of their role in the process because they know their views are taken very seriously by the panel charged with making the appointment. Candidates spend lunch-time with the staff, who subsequently relay their views back to the SMT. A Teaching Assistant (TA) is given the job of welcoming and looking after all candidates during the day and her views are also sought during the final deliberations.

We have discovered that a careful selection of questions is crucial in the interview. After standard questions relating to their professional experience we ask about the candidates' goals in life, their personal strategies for overcoming difficulties and their understanding about what it will mean for them to be part of a Church school that is underpinned by Christian values. We often ask focused questions such as "Is there a value that we have not included in our list that is especially important to you?".

Making this conscious decision to include our school values as a focus for our appointment process has transformed a procedure that was frequently frustrating and sometimes unsuccessful. We now have real confidence in our system and two recent appointments of Teaching Assistants serve as good examples of the effectiveness of the new process. Both Ellie and Sophie have added hugely to the life of St. Mary's in the short time that they have been with us. Neither had specific TA qualifications when they were appointed but both have brought a genuine commitment to our ethos and their gifts and abilities have benefitted all the children in the school.

Sophie runs a drama club with the expressed purpose of raising self-esteem in children who have been identified as lacking confidence.

Sophie runs a drama club with the expressed purpose of raising self-esteem in children who have been identified as lacking confidence.

For Sophie working at St. Marys has confirmed for her the next step in her career path. "When I left university I was not totally sure what I wanted to do, but having seen the positive impact and influence that a good teacher can have on children I am now convinced that it is right to apply to do a PGCE."

Ellie leads a music ensemble for children who are gifted musicians and this group is now working on writing a 'Values' song for the whole school. Ellie has decided to train as a music therapist. "Seeing how music can be creatively used to bring out the very best in children has been an inspiration."

The appointments have been hugely successful from the school's perspective, but I was curious to know about Ellie's own reflections on her year at St. Mary's school.

What initially attracted you to apply for a post at St. Mary's?

This post stood out for me for several reasons; its one-on-one nature with a child with SEN; emphasis placed on both the child and family; being part of a staff team where relationships were clearly rooted in values and the school's Christian foundation. My hope was that a Church school would encourage an atmosphere and behaviour that reflected consideration for others, a strong moral framework and space to develop the children's spirituality. These factors, coupled with my personal faith, made the St. Mary's post one that I was excited to apply for.

How did the interview process help you to know if the school was right for you?

The moment I arrived at the school, I was met by a TA who made me feel comfortable and welcome. I remember a display of 'friendship spoons' in the entrance that embodied the emphasis on love and the value of each individual

Children have often come to tell me they have "shown perseverance" or that "someone has shown kindness to me".

that I had hoped to find. Therefore, before I had even got to interview, I felt at home. During the formal interview certain questions stood out. Why did I want this post? How did I feel about working in a school with Christian values? Could I tell about a time when I had achieved something difficult and how I set about it? What did I think was my biggest weakness in applying for this post? I felt that I was able to demonstrate aspects of my character and experience that shaped and motivated me, rather than merely discuss my knowledge of the workings of primary schools.

What difference does it make to work at a school with Christian Values at its heart?

Prior to my employment at St. Mary's I expected that a faith school would encourage expression of core moral values. What I have found fascinating is the way St. Mary's has sought to embody these in all areas of school life. As the children are enabled to explore the values through worship and class discussion, their understanding of,

for example, what it means to love one another, to have high self-esteem and to respect all people, is both deep and practical. Children on the playground have often come to tell me they have "shown perseverance" or that "someone has shown kindness to me". Through these values comes one of the key messages of the Bible: that everyone is special and immeasurably precious, and we are to treat everyone with care. A Year 5 boy told me that respect is "showing people that you know they're there". However it is not just in the learning or relationships between children I have seen the values manifest, but also among staff in their planning, their view of the children, the leadership dynamic and the culture of concern for one another. At St. Mary's there is something reminiscent of a family structure that has arisen from the practical application of the values in school.

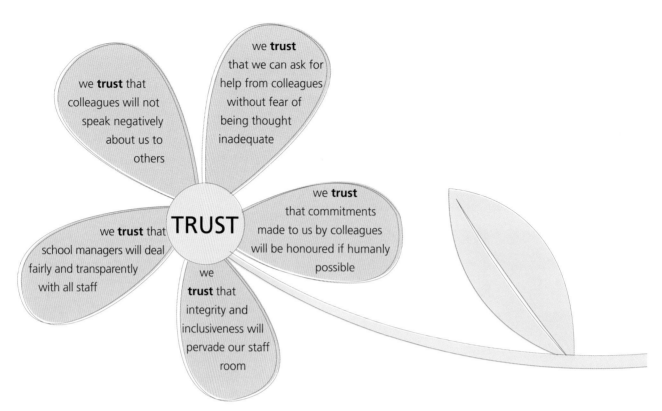

We have found that building an effective staff team that is able to model these values and lead by example is absolutely key.

It is clear that the early days of being part of a new team can be crucial in determining how staff settle in and find their feet. Recently, in order to help members of staff with this process we asked a relatively new teacher to draft an induction booklet. The purpose of this document was to give a newcomer's perspective on the workings of the school, to highlight day to day practices, and to outline the fundamental importance of our values on how we live and work together. This has been a valuable addition to our Welcome Pack. Another school that I know has asked members of staff to try and describe in practical terms what each of the values means to the way they as adults relate to one another. This is reviewed regularly at staff meetings and has been extremely challenging and a powerful tool for mutual accountability.

New teachers at St. Mary's are guided by a professional mentor who helps them with their action plan and meeting the Teaching Standards. In addition, they have a buddy who is a more informal and pastoral point of contact. Younger members of staff have found this especially helpful as they settle into a new place of work, sometimes a long way from family and existing support networks.

When a school claims to have Christian values at its heart, it is vital that these values genuinely permeate all aspects of the life of the school. At St. Mary's we have found that building an effective staff team which is able to model these values and lead by example is absolutely key to this process.

VALUES: INFORMING POLICY

If Christian values underpin the life of a school, those values will form the starting point for all policy development. When Diocesan Schools' Advisers Verity Holloway and Katy Staples together with Kate Guthrie from Hope's Place, a Bristol based pregnancy crisis charity, responded to requests from schools for a resource to support sex and relationship education (SRE) they began by considering the values that would inform their work. The publication that has resulted from their collaboration is *Love and Sex Matters.* In this chapter Verity gives a flavour of its contents.

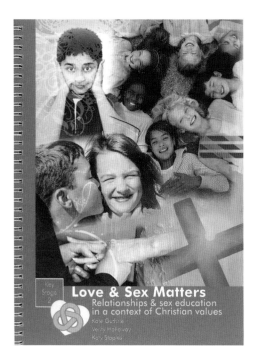
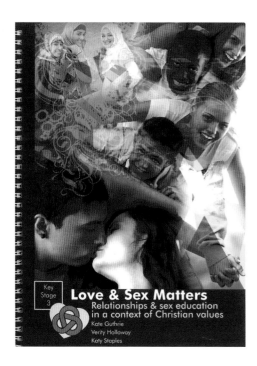

We asked what relationships might look like in practice when forgiveness, hope or justice are the lenses through which they are viewed.

At present Britain has the highest rate of teenage pregnancy in Europe and the most common sexually transmitted infection, chlamydia, has seen a 150% rise over the past five years. With these rather startling statistics as a backdrop and in response to the recommendations from the Good Childhood Report[1] about children's contemporary experiences of growing up, Katy Staples, Kate Guthrie and I formed a working group to write a practical resource for teaching SRE which took as its starting point the values which underpin all that is central to our relationships in Church schools.

First we looked at each of the core values from *Values for Life* and devised a set of questions that might arise when teaching SRE. We asked what relationships might look like in practice when forgiveness, hope or justice are the lenses through which they are viewed. These are some of the questions we identified:

FORGIVENESS

- When should I say sorry?
- How do I say sorry?
- Why do I need to receive forgiveness?
- How do I know when I should forgive?
- What changes when I forgive?
- How do I forgive myself?
- How do I know that I am forgiven?

HOPE

- What do I hope for?
- What makes me feel hopeless?
- Where do I see hope in the world?
- Who gives me hope?
- How can I give hope to others?

SERVICE

- What are my special gifts?
- How can I use these gifts to serve others?
- Does serving others mean that I do not assert myself?

1 A Good Childhood: Searching for values in a competitive age. Report published Dec 2009 by The Children's Society

2 Love & Sex Matters, publ. The Salisbury Diocese Board of Education 2010

Love and Sex Matters...gives opportunities to rehearse appropriate language when discussing relationships.

With these values and their implications for all our relationships as a bedrock for our work we drew up the following set of aims for the new publications. *Love & Sex Matters*[2] will:

- Offer exciting, fun and interactive lessons in which values and beliefs can be explored in relation to sexuality and relationships.

- Give opportunities to rehearse appropriate language when discussing relationships and develop articulacy.

- Build self-esteem and high regard for others; in church schools this is rooted in a belief that all are loved by God.

- Uphold the sanctity of marriage and the importance of long-term relationships and stable family life.

- Offer views from a variety of Christian perspectives, from other faiths and from non-religious life perspectives.

- Enable children and young people to question messages in the media and advertising about body image and sexuality.

Conscious that teachers had expressed the wish that this resource should provide practical outlines of suggested lessons, we decided to write four books for the first four key stages, each one containing a series of eight lessons dealing with different aspects of SRE in an age appropriate context.

The following page shows a grid of lessons included in the Key Stage 2 publication.

Lesson	Summary	Learning Outcomes
1. Making me	Pupils will think about the factors that contribute to an identity and what makes someone valuable.	• I can describe what makes me 'me'. • I can explain why all people are valuable, including me.
2. My world, your world	Pupils will think about how their lives interact with other people's lives and how this affects decision-making.	• I can explain ways in which what I do might affect other people emotionally and /or physically. • I can identify the people whose lives might be changed by what I do. • I can explain how recognising how my actions influence other people can help me make good decisions.
3. Changing bodies	Pupils will think about the physical and emotional changes that take place during puberty.	• I can describe how I will change physically and emotionally during puberty.
4. Firm foundations	Pupils will think about what provides firm foundations for a relationship and how awareness of this might affect whom they date.	• I can describe characteristics that will help build a good relationship and why these are important. • I can explain what sort of things I might look for in a friend or partner and why.
5. Marriage	Pupils will reflect on the significance and meaning of the wedding service and marriage and how these benefit the individual and the community.	• I can explain why Christians think marriage is important. • I can explain how marriage is good for relationships within the family and in the wider community.
6. Great expectations?	Pupils will think about the meaning of sex and why it is best kept for marriage or long-term relationships.	• I can explain what I think is normal sexual behaviour. • I can describe what some religions think about sex. • I can give reasons why it might be good to keep sex for marriage or a long-term, committed relationship.
7. In need of restoration?	Pupils will think about the role of forgiveness in sustaining and deepening relationships.	• I can explain why it is good to forgive people. • I can describe some situations when I think you should or should not show forgiveness and explain why.
8. Summary activities	Activities to draw course together and encourage pupils to reflect on what they have learnt.	• I can consider what makes a relationship 'life-giving' or 'life-limiting'. • I can describe actions that would make my relationships more 'life-giving'.

In a Conscience Alley activity children explore reasons for and against offering forgiveness.

Each lesson includes some introductory reflective prompts for discussion followed by a number of learning activities designed to encourage pupils to explore the issues surrounding the lesson focus. Extension questions are included to develop thinking at a deeper level which broadens pupils understanding of forgiveness. For example in the lesson *In Need of Restoration?*, the extension questions are:

- Does forgiving someone mean pretending an event never happened?

- Some actions have permanent, negative consequences - do you think such actions would be harder to forgive?

At the end of each lesson is a plenary activity designed to focus and reinforce learning. In Lesson 7 this takes the form of a Conscience Alley activity, *see below*.

Scenario

My parents have decided that I have to move schools, even though I really don't want to. Their only reason is that it is closer to home. Can/should I forgive them?

- In this activity pupils will think about whether everything is forgivable or whether it is sometimes OK not to forgive.
- Divide the class into two equal sized groups.
- In each group ask one pupil to be a particular character and give them the scenario to read.
- Ask the remaining pupils in the group to form two lines that face each other, making an 'alley'.
- The scenario character should read out the situation to his/her group and then begin to walk slowly down the alley.
- As the character proceeds, each person in the line must explain out loud in one sentence why they think the character should or should not forgive.
- At the end bring the whole class back together.
- Ask both characters to explain briefly their situation and then whether or not they want to forgive the people who have hurt them. Ask them to explain what has influenced this decision.
- Ask the class for their response: How many of the group agree with their decisions? How many do not? Why / why not? Do you think that some things are unforgiveable?

Included in the volumes are a number of appendices. One of these is a Sex and Relationship Education policy which makes explicit the underpinning values and principles.

Sample Sex and Relationships Education policy from Love & Sex Matters Key Stage 2

Introduction

Sex education is part of the personal, social and health education curriculum in our school. We will teach within a framework of Christian values and the Christian understanding that sex is a gift of God as part of creation. Whilst we use sex education to inform children about sexual issues, we do this with regard to matters of morality and individual responsibility, and in a way that allows children to ask and explore moral questions. Sensitivity and respect should be shown to all children when teaching about personal relationships and sex education and SRE should be taught in a way to ensure that there is no stigmatization of children based on their home/personal circumstances.

Context

All SRE in a Church of England school should be set in a context which is consistent with the school's Christian ethos and values.

- SRE should be based on inclusive Christian principles and values, emphasising respect, compassion, loving care and forgiveness.
- SRE should be taught in the light of the belief in the absolute worth of all people and the unconditional, infinite love of God.
- SRE should reflect that sex is a gift from God as part of creation: a human longing for intimate union.
- SRE should be sensitive to the circumstances of all children and be mindful of the variety of expressions of family life in our culture, yet it should also uphold the Christian values regarding relationships and marriage.
- Issues regarding human sexuality should be addressed sensitively.
- The exploration of reproduction and sexual behaviour within the science curriculum should stand alongside the exploration of relationships, values and morals and Christian belief.

Whilst pupils are given the opportunity to explore their own attitudes, values and beliefs and to develop an individual moral code that will guide their actions, this is exercised within an understanding of the right of people to hold their own views within a framework of respect for others.

Aims and objectives

We teach children about:

- The physical development of their bodies as they grow into adults;
- The way humans reproduce;
- Respect for their own bodies and the importance of sexual activity as part of a committed, long-term and loving relationship;
- The importance of marriage and family life;
- Values questions;
- Relationship issues;
- Respect for the views of other people;
- What they should do if they are worried about any sexual matters.

The following sections are also included in the sample policy.

Principles

Organisation

The role of parents

The role of other members of the community

Confidentiality and safeguarding children procedures

The role of the headteacher

Monitoring and review

VALUES: COLLECTIVE WORSHIP

David Crunkhurn has been headteacher at Westbury-on-Severn Voluntary Aided Church of England School for 2 years. He is a member of the local SACRE (Standing Advisory Council for Religious Education) and also serves on the Gloucester Diocesan Board of Education. David writes about how Values themes can enrich Collective Worship linking spiritual and moral development in ways that are both innovative and inspirational.

At the beginning of the new term the staff meet to discuss the intended learning outcomes that will result from our whole school focus on the value.

Planning for Collective Worship in the following term is initially done in conjunction with a neighbouring Church school because we share the same vicar and Ministry Team. We use the *Values for Life* resource as the starting point for our planning. This gives everyone involved in leading worship in our two schools a focus and framework. We look at the core Bible stories suggested for the term as well as the story texts, poems, music and other resources. Having this meeting well in advance gives us time to purchase additional materials to support the theme or to borrow them from the Diocesan Resource Library. At the beginning of the new term the staff meet to discuss the intended learning outcomes that will result from our whole school focus on the value. Lunch time supervisors and foundation governors are invited to this staff meeting to ensure we are all *singing from the same hymn sheet!* We use the questions outlined at the start of each chapter in *Values for Life* to initiate this discussion.

For *Humility* this term the questions included:

- In what ways do we encourage all members of the school community to serve one another?

- How do we encourage pupils to be empathetic and sympathetic to the experiences of others?

- How do we create an ethos in which children and adults are confident to ask for help and to receive help from others?

Our School Worship Team made up from children representing all year groups also meets to plan their acts of worship. These always turn out to be very creative and include dance/drama as well as the children's own musical compositions.

Weekly Programme

Monday

The Key Note worship is led by me. It includes the core Bible story and sets the scene for worship in the week ahead.

Prayer: Please God, help us to be humble enough to ask for help when we need it.

Key Note Worship from Values for Life
Value: Humility

Week 2: Humility to seek help
In this act of worship children hear the story from Luke 7 of the Roman soldier who asked Jesus to heal his servant. They reflect on the Christian understanding that, at times, we all need the humility to ask for help and a willingness to accept help from others.

Whole School Worship

Visual Focus: *box of PE equipment where items have been put back in the wrong place and are very muddled up.*
Music: *Beethoven Pastoral Symphony*
Song: *Father I place into your hands*

Introduction: Worship leader: Ask for a volunteer who is willing to take on a challenge. Ask them to sort the PE equipment box so that all skipping ropes are together, all tennis balls together, etc. As he or she begins sorting ask the other children what might make the job quicker and easier. Allow the volunteer to choose someone to help them.

Explain to the children that there are many situations in life when we need to ask for help. Ask them to think about and respond to the question: What sometimes stops us from asking for help? Ask the children to reflect upon what would happen if they didn't ask for help in the following circumstances:

• they are going somewhere new and need directions

• they don't understand their work in school

• they don't know how a toy or game works.

Explain that we are going to hear a story about an important person who had the humility to ask Jesus for help.

Text: 'A Soldiers Faith' (Lion Bible for Children retold by Murray Watts)

Development: The soldier realised that he needed help. He also knew that the way in which he asked for help was important. We all need to ask for help at times. Christians believe that through prayer God hears us and helps us.

Prayer: Please God, help us to be humble enough to ask for help when we need it and show us how we can be a help to others. Amen.

Each class has a Worship Box which contains a collection of cloths, artefacts, candles and Bible story books.

Tuesday

Once a week Key Stage 1 and Key Stage 2 meet separately for worship. Key Stage 2 may use a story from current affairs that demonstrates the value in focus being worked out locally, nationally or globally. Sometimes our School Worship Team lead this service. Key Stage 1 have been piloting a new resource, The Values Worship Chest[1], designed especially for younger children. This uses a wicker hamper and drape to create a *sacred space* in the classroom.

The drape, the colour of which is determined by the liturgical colour of the church season, is taken from the hamper and a short liturgy *(see opposite)* is used which children learn. There then follows a story on the theme of the value and a concluding prayer.

Wednesday

Our local clergy and ministry team lead worship each week either using one of the supplementary Bible stories suggested in *Values for Life* or taking a theme relevant to the church season.

Thursday

Class Worship – each class teacher leads worship, using an idea from the 'Taking The Theme a Step Further' section of the *Values for Life* programme. Here are two examples from the value *Humility*:

• Key Stage 1 - Read some stories in which one character is boastful or arrogant, e.g. Hare and Tortoise from Aesop's fables.

• Key Stage 2 - Make a before and after chart for the story of Joseph (Genesis 37-50) using words which describe how his attitude changed through his life experiences.

Each class has a Worship Box which contains a collection of cloths, artefacts, candles and Bible story books that the teacher and children have built up over time. This helps to create a visual focus and a sense of the sacred in the middle of a busy classroom.

Friday

At the end of the week we hold a Celebration Worship, during which individual children are praised for exemplifying the value in focus by their behaviour throughout the week. We always have lots of singing in Friday worship and I try to choose songs which are about the Bible stories that the values for the term are rooted in. For many of our children, school is the only place they hear Bible stories so we use music to help them become really memorable.

1 The Values Worship Chest, Publication 2012

The Values Worship Chest

Value: Trust
Jesus heals the blind man John 9

Opening Liturgy

Leader: Today we open the Worship Chest and spread out the colour purple.

Leader: We take out a candle and light it to remind us that...

Children: *God's love burns brightly for each one of us.*

Leader: We take out the cross and place it at the centre to remind us that...

Children: *Jesus is at the centre of our school.*

Leader: We take out the Bible and open it to remind us that...

Children: *God speaks to us through his word.*

Introduction

Our eyes are very precious and beautiful.

We use them to see the wonderful world that God has created for us to enjoy.

In the box are some amazing things for us to look at.

Here is a feather from a bird. It is a special shape. It helps the bird to fly and keeps it warm and dry.

Here is a flower from my garden. It is bright and colourful to attract the insects.

Here is a picture of the faces of people special to me. Who is special to you?

Story

One day, when Jesus was out walking with his friends he came upon a man who had never been able to see. He had been born blind. The man's neighbours helped him when they could, but still the man had to beg for money to buy his food. When Jesus saw the man he felt so sorry that he stopped and bent down beside him. Jesus then did a strange but wonderful thing. He made some soft mud with the brown soil and carefully wiped it on the eyelids of the blind man. "Now go and wash in the pool of Siloam" Jesus told him. The man **trusted** Jesus. He knew that Jesus wanted to help him. As the man splashed the cool water onto his face, something miraculous happened. He began to see splashes of sparkling light on the surface of the water. As he looked up, for the very first time he saw birds amongst the leaves in the branches of the trees above his head. He looked down and saw bright flowers at his feet. And all around the man saw the faces of the neighbours that he had known all his life. Some of the neighbours could hardly believe what they saw. But others laughed and danced for joy, because they knew that a miracle had happened. Their friend had **trusted** Jesus and Jesus had healed him.

Prayer with responses

Leader: The response to our prayer today is "Thank you Father God".

Leader: For our eyes and the gift of sight,
Children: *Thank you Father God.*

Leader: For birds and flowers and faces,
Children: *Thank you Father God.*

Leader: For those we **trust** who care about us and help us,
Children: *Thank you Father God.*

Everyone: Amen
(Blow out candle to signify the end of the act of worship)

	DATE	PRAYER FOCUS	DATE	PRAYER FOCUS
PATHWAYS TO PRAYER	1st	Head Teacher	16th	The street where you live
	2nd	Bright Horizons and families	17th	People who run school clubs
	3rd	Reception and their families	18th	People in our family
	4th	Cleaning staff	19th	Adults who help in school
	5th	Year 1 and their families	20th	Our friends
	6th	Teaching support staff	21st	Our Family Support Worker
	7th	Year 2 and their families	22nd	The Friends of Westbury School
	8th	Teachers	23rd	Our Vicar
	9th	Year 3 and their families	24th	Westbury Village businesses
	10th	Midday supervisors	25th	Our World
	11th	Year 4 and their families	26th	Ourselves
	12th	Mrs Cox	27th	People we know who are ill
	13th	Year 5 and their families	28th	The church family
	14th	School Governors	29th	Friends who have moved away
	15th	Year 6 and their families	30th	Ex pupils now in secondary school

Children are invited to place a red bead in the bowl if they wish to offer a prayer of thanksgiving, a blue bead for a prayer to say sorry...

Prayer

Prayer is not just at the heart of our times of Collective Worship but it undergirds everything that we do. We try to make it as accessible and interactive as possible for both adults and children. We do this is in a number of ways:

Pathways to Prayer cards
These break down the month into 30 days, each day having a focus for prayer which relates to the life of the school. *(See example above)*. These cards are given to everyone in the school community including parents.

Prayer Stations
There are reflective prayer stations in our entrance area and in each classroom, so that there is always a quiet space for children to spend time in.

Prayer Times during the day
As well as morning acts of worship, specific times to pray are set aside each day at lunch-time and home-time. Prayers are written by the children or chosen by them from published prayer books.

Rainbow Prayers
I have adopted an excellent idea from Ashleworth CE School which helps the children to appreciate the range of different kinds of prayers. A transparent bowl is surrounded by five plastic tumblers containing coloured beads. Children are invited to place a red bead in the bowl if they wish to offer a prayer of thanksgiving, a blue bead for a prayer to say sorry, a yellow bead for a prayer for others, an orange bead for a prayer for the world or a white bead to offer a prayer for themselves.

A Prayer Wall
Post-it Notes are placed near the prayer wall so that children and adults can write short prayers which will be included in the worship in school, in the parish church and in the intercessions of the school's parent prayer group.

Prayers for the Church Year
Being a Church of England school we have special prayers appropriate to the church calendar. For these we use *Prayers for Life* published by Jumping Fish Ltd.

VALUES: SPIRITUAL DEVELOPMENT

St. Paul's Voluntary Controlled Church of England Primary School is a vibrant, inner city, multi-cultural school situated near to the docks in Gloucester. Hayley Hutchison took up the post of Headteacher in September 2006. In this chapter she describes how her school uses the Windows Mirrors and Doors strategy as a structure for developing spirituality in the school through their values themes.

Together we decided that the re-establishment of the Church of England distinctiveness in the school should be a priority.

On being appointed Headteacher of St. Paul's I knew that I faced a number of difficult challenges but this was brought home very clearly when, just two weeks after I arrived, the school was placed in Special Measures by Ofsted. As well as issues around standards, I was concerned that the expression of St. Paul's as a Church of England School was generally very understated.

It was a real encouragement when Revd Ricarda Witcombe walked into school having just been licensed as vicar of the parish. Together we decided that the re-establishment of the Church of England distinctiveness in the school should be a priority. After a huge amount of commitment and hard work on both our parts, together with support from a committed staff team, in March 2008 the school was removed from Special Measures and graded as 'good'. We went from strength to strength and in May 2010 we were judged 'Good with some outstanding features' by Ofsted. One such feature was behaviour and we are in no doubt that the introduction of

the *Values for Life* programme contributed to the judgement. We were equally delighted to be judged 'good' in the SIAS inspection.

One of the focii for development, identified by SIAS was to "Review the school's interpretation of spirituality so that it includes all aspects of life in school."

In order to address this we invited Shahne Vickery, our Diocesan Primary Adviser, to lead an INSET with all staff, to help us think strategically about strengthening this area of our school life. First she asked us to think about how we would define spirituality in a way that would be inclusive of the wide range of religious faiths and cultures represented by children in our community. She offered us a number of definitions, written by a range of theologians and educational bodies, to consider and discuss. We chose aspects of several of those that we wanted to include in a statement that we felt expressed a working definition of spirituality that resonated with us all.

We wanted our values to somehow be a framework for the way we explored spirituality.

Shahne then asked us to consider the kinds of characteristics that we would be seeking to encourage in our pupils to help them to become more confident in their own spirituality. These were some of the suggestions from staff:

- Self respect and respect for others

- A sense of adventure and willingness to try new things

- Curiosity about the natural world

- Confidence in our own beliefs with an openness to learning from other ways of thinking

- Imagination and creativity

- Fearlessness about asking the *big questions*

- A willingness to look *below the surface*

- A keen awareness of injustice

- Being comfortable with mystery

- An ability to stand in another's shoes and look at things from their perspective

During the last few years we have worked hard to embed everything that we do in our Christian values. We therefore wanted our values to somehow be a framework for the way we explored spirituality. At this point Shahne introduced us to the work of Liz Mills who has created three visual images, *windows, mirrors* and *doors*, for thinking about different ways of expressing spirituality *(see overleaf)*.

The teachers found these images really helpful because we have tended to focus a lot on awe and wonder but miss out other kinds of spirituality especially thinking about the painful moments and how we grow through them. We also felt that we were not adequately supporting our children in their questioning about some of the mysteries that we live with as human beings, questions such as "How do I know God loves me?" and "When my Grandpa died where did he go?" or "Why did a loving God create my cat in a way that she tortures the mice she catches?".

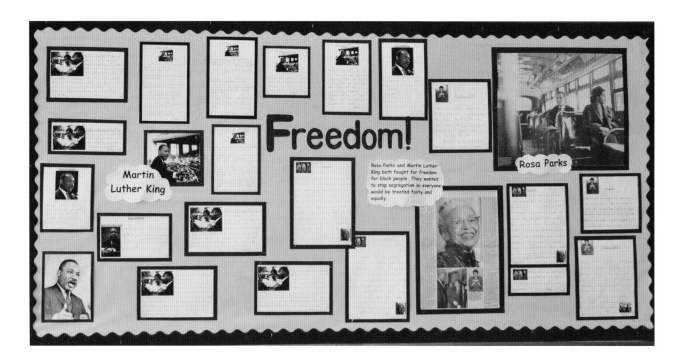

It was suggested that we take our school values and discuss what a Window, Mirror and Door task might look like for each of them.

The Windows, Mirrors and Doors strategy

In the following text Liz Mills describes how the images work:

WINDOWS: giving children opportunities to become *aware* of the world in new ways; to **wonder** about life's 'Wows' (things that are amazing) and 'Ows' (things that bring us up short). In this children are learning *about* life in all its fullness.

MIRRORS: giving children opportunities to *reflect* on their experiences; to **meditate** on life's big questions and to consider some possible answers. In this they are learning *from* life by exploring their own insights and perspectives and those of others.

DOORS: giving children opportunities to *respond* to all of this; to **do** something creative as a means of expressing, applying and further developing their thoughts and convictions. In this they are learning to *live* by putting into action what they are coming to believe and value.

©Liz Mills Farmington Millennium Research 1997

It was suggested that we take our school values and discuss in groups what a Window, Mirror and Door task might look like for each of them.

Below are some of our ideas:

Courage

W – identify and gain inspiration and motivation from the courage shown by others

M –reflect on how and where people find the courage to face huge challenges

D – take action to step outside our comfort zone.

Forgiveness

W – to find inspiration in the transforming effect of being forgiven and given a new start

M – reflect on why some people believe it important to ask God for forgiveness and consider if this is important for us

D - take an initiative in forgiving someone that has wronged us in some way.

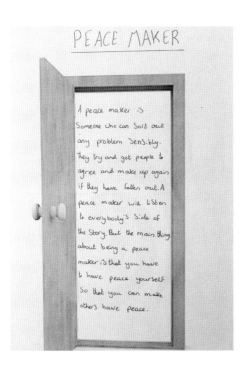

Peace Maker

A peace maker is

Someone who can sort out any problem sensibly.

They try and get people to agree and make up again if they have fallen out.

A peace maker will listen to everybody's side of the story.

But the main thing about being a peace maker is that you have to have peace yourself so that you can make others have peace.

Each child thought about which qualities make a good peacemaker

During the final part of the INSET each member of staff took their planning for next term and looked for Windows, Mirrors and Doors opportunities across the curriculum. We then got together with our Key Stage colleagues to discuss our ideas.

The day really galvanised the staff. The great thing about this strategy was that even teachers who lacked confidence in this area felt that there was now a common understanding for approaching spiritual development throughout the school that everyone could grasp.

The children's work represents some of the ways that the different classes explored the value *Peace* using the Windows, Mirrors and Doors strategy.

Window
Year 2 learnt about how Martin Luther King fought discrimination and prejudice by peaceful, not violent, means.

Mirror
Year 1 explored Mirror Moments to consider what peace meant to them. At this age the children were thinking in more concrete terms and gave examples from the domestic context. Using the texts *Peace at Last* and *Five Minutes Peace* by Gill Murphy the children talked about the kinds of behaviour that make for a noisy home and a quiet home and how parents and carers react to this. The children drew noisy, hectic home scenes and peaceful, quiet ones.

Door
Year 4 looked at causes of conflict and disharmony at break and lunchtimes in school and considered the impact of peacemakers in the playground, in the form of our peer mediators. Each child thought about which qualities make a good peacemaker and considered whether they might one day wish to be trained as a peer mediator.

Each school that operates a Peer Mediation Scheme does so in a way that works successfully in their context. However there are general principals that are common to all schemes. These are outlined below:

What is a Peer Mediator?

A peer mediator is a person who has been taught to help fellow pupils sort out arguments. The mediator listens as each person who has been part of the disagreement tells their side of the story and guides discussion to reach an agreement on how to sort out the problem. He/she does not take sides and doesn't tell everyone else what has been said, in other words they keep what is said private. The mediator guides the discussion, but does not decide the outcome.

A peer mediator needs to be:

• A good listener

• Patient and caring with others

• Good at co-operating

• Able to keep things private

• Sensitive to other's feelings

How to set up Peer Mediation

When setting up a peer mediation scheme in a primary school, the teachers will normally train a group of pupils in a series of one hour workshops. The training has generally worked best with Year 5 children because they will be in the school for a whole year following training and have the opportunity to use their skills. The workshops teach listening skills, communication skills, co-operation and the peer mediation process through games, role plays and discussions. The whole class could do the workshop activities and learn skills that are useful even if children attending never become actual mediators. After the course the leader will ask for volunteers to become mediators. For those who take on the mediation role parental permission must be sought for their work.

How Peer Mediation works

Anyone who wants to come for mediation can simply approach a peer mediator on duty or can be asked to fill in a form asking for help. Once this is done the peer mediators will decide on a venue for the meeting. Normally they are encouraged to mediate in the playground, spiritual garden or in a quiet reflection space inside at break or lunchtime, but always near an adult just in case help is needed.

They work in pairs and follow a series of steps:

• Agree to mediate and set out ground rules such as no interrupting, no accusations, no name calling

• Find out both sides of the story – listening carefully and finding out how each person feels

• List the problems that need to be sorted out

• Suggest possible ideas for an agreement

• Settle the agreement and write a summary to remind each person what has been said

• Ask each person to shake hands to seal the agreement.

Resolution through mediation

Issues that involve peer mediators tend to revolve around lack of co-operation, conflict exacerbated by stubbornness, back biting and failure to say sorry or hurt feelings. In all situations the peer mediators can remind everyone of the school values and how these are lived out in practice and encourage everyone to work together, share ideas, listen to alternative points of view and talk about emotions and feelings. A successful resolution is one in which everyone feels they have been fairly treated.

VALUES: ACROSS THE CURRICULUM

Before becoming Schools' Adviser in the Diocese of Gloucester, Shahne Vickery worked as a class teacher and Deputy Head in Primary Schools in Wales. In recent years she has written a number of popular titles including Pause for Reflection, Creating a Multi-sensory Spiritual Garden and Experience Easter. Shahne is perhaps best known for her work on Values Education and in this chapter looks at opportunities for teaching values across a range of curriculum areas.

Where values run through a school like the writing through a stick of seaside rock, there will be a conscious commitment by teachers to link them to each area of the curriculum.

In the first chapter of this book Margaret James from St. Mary's Primary School, Thornbury writes, 'Although values were important themes in Collective Worship they seemed to have become add-ons rather than principles informing our school's vision and aims and underpinning how we live together as a community.'

This school is not alone in recognising that the values messages enthusiastically and creatively delivered in assembly and worship are not necessarily being seen by everyone as relevant back in class. One new headteacher said that her staff were astonished when, during a focus on the value *Respect* she suggested an appropriate response might be that neither children or staff should be spoken of negatively in the staffroom!

Where values run through a school like the writing through a stick of seaside rock, there will be a conscious commitment by teachers to link them to each area of the curriculum. Included in the Introduction to the publication *Values for Life* there is an extensive list suggesting ways in which each curriculum area might contribute to the development of values.

For example:

PE offers children opportunities to:
- Consider issues of fairness and morality in the context of games and sport
- Learn to trust themselves and others

Maths offers children opportunities to:
- Be creative thinkers as they apply mathematical skills in solving problems such as how much rubbish does our school generate or how many litres of water do we use in one day?
- Begin to understand how statistics that are used to justify a position can sometimes present a misleading impression

History offers children opportunities to:
- Appreciate how situations of injustice have provoked men and women to rise up and often, against all the odds, bring change and transformation

Science offers children opportunities to:
- Appreciate that in order to investigate fairly, commitment and honest observation are crucial.

Children from the Cotswold View cluster of schools in Gloucestershire created a forest sculpture as part of a focus on Respect and Reverence for creation. The piece is called Prayers for the World.

Art offers children opportunities to:
- Interpret values through a range of creative media

- Discern the 'values messages' being communicated through the work of artists and designers

Some schools have included discreet lessons on the timetable for Values Education. A number of strategies are used to stimulate discussion and exploration.

- **News items** and contemporary stories in the news provide a powerful way of discussing values being lived out (or not) on the local, national or international stage;

- **Real life dilemmas**, explored for example through a conscience alley activity *(see p. 33)*;

- **Fictional or Traditional Stories**, such as Aesop's Fables or myths and legends, which demonstrate how moral dilemmas are not a new phenomenon!

- **Wisdom Texts**, such as Biblical proverbs which can be used as a stimulus for drama or creative writing;

- **Pictures or photographs**, which resonate with children and provoke discussion;

- **Film and Television excerpts**, which when shown in a context of values education can encourage children to consider critically messages that they otherwise might miss.

The examples included on the following pages are from schools which have used values as a stimulus in a variety of contexts. The first shows the RE curriculum planning from a school in Bristol which took a unit of work on *Justice* and *Compassion*.

Unit of work in RE
Key Stage 2
Local Study

Step 1. Select key question	**How do the values justice and compassion influence the lives of local Christians and impact community life?** *Where does this fit into our Key Stage planning?* This unit is designed to be taught as part of our whole school focus on the values justice and compassion in terms 5 and 6. We will identify opportunities for teaching these values across the curriculum. In Collective Worship we will use Values for Life as our core resource, children will be learning about: the work of Christian Aid; the Jubilee Debt Campaign; the story of Jonah (Jonah 1-4); the Feeding of the 5,000 (Matthew 14); the story of Ruth and Naomi from Ruth 1; the Good Samaritan (Luke 10); the story of Dorcas (Acts 9).
Step 2. Select learning outcomes	This unit looks at the impact of the values justice and compassion in the lives of Christians and through them in the local context. We will focus on one young Christian, MB, and his local church's response to the problem of debt in the area. We are therefore focusing on the following outcomes, applying the learning to Christianity. • *Identify* personal, family, school values which influence children's own behaviour • *Explain* why justice and compassion are important values for Christians (making reference to relevant stories from the Bible). • *Explore* why the values justice and compassion inform Christians' sense of duty, and why they seek to serve their community. • *Ask and respond to questions* about having a set of values to guide choices and decisions in daily life.
Step 3. Select specific content	• Teachings which act as guides for living within Christianity, e.g. the parables of the Unforgiving Debtor (Matthew 18: 21-35) (justice) and the Good Samaritan (Luke 10:25-37) (compassion). • The importance of values as guides for making choices and decisions in daily life. • The value and challenge for believers of following a code for living. • What guides pupils' own moral choices? Extra content selected: • Reflection on our school values and how they influence our behaviour • The values of a local Christian teenager, and how these led him to support a debt counselling charity by running the Bristol half-marathon • The values of church members in establishing a debt counselling centre in their community.

Step 4. Assessment: levelled pupil outcomes	These learning outcomes are turned into levelled "I can…" statements in the teaching and learning activities below. **Level 3** I can identify which values are important in our school community, and explain how they influence our behaviour. I can make links between the teachings of Jesus, and why justice and compassion are important for Christians. I can make links between the values held by local Christians and their service to the community. I can describe the impact of a local project run by Christians on the lives of individuals within our community. I can identify values that are important to me, and say how they influence the way I behave. **Level 4** I can identify which values are important in our school community, giving examples of how they have informed school policy and decision-making, e.g. our Behaviour Policy and the charities we support as a school. I can give modern day interpretations of some of Jesus' parables about justice and compassion. I can recognise that people of different faiths, and no religious faith, share the values justice and compassion, but have a variety of reasons for holding these values. I can explain the impact of a local project run by Christians on the lives of individuals, and the broader impact of this within our community. I can identify values that are important to me, and recognise ways in which these are sometimes counter-cultural.

Step 5. Learning opportunities	• Devise a questionnaire to use with children in other classes to establish whether they can identify the school values and how far they have made a difference to behaviour in the school.
	• Dramatise the two key parables for the unit, i.e. The Unforgiving Debtor and the Good Samaritan, and hot-seat characters to explore the values that motivated Jesus to tell these stories.
	• Create contemporary interpretations to the parables, which illustrate the underlying values.
	• Interview MB to find out why his core values motivated him to undertake training for the Bristol half-marathon to raise funds for his church's debt counselling centre.
	Search the CAP website http://www.capuk.org to discover the following:
	  o What motivated the founder of the debt counselling charity Christians Against Poverty (CAP) to establish this organisation?
	  o How does CAP help people out of debt?
	  o How does it work in partnership with churches to serve local communities?
	  o What impact does the local CAP Centre have on the lives of individual families?
	
	• Interview a CAP client to find out how CAP has helped him to manage debt and reflect on how his values have changed through their experience.
	
	• Use a *Diamond 9* activity to explore whether the children think a 'values hierarchy' exists (children arrange the values according to their opinion of their importance, giving their reasons e.g. wisdom at the top, courage and friendship underneath etc.). *See page 22.*

Children in the Reception class need lots of stories to help them understand what the value looks like in practice.

Value: Perseverance
Topic: Safe and Sound
Year group - Reception
Class Teacher - Mrs Ridler

As part of the topic, Safe and Sound, the Reception class at St. Paul's C of E School in Gloucester was learning about the story of Mary Seacole. The whole school value in focus was *Perseverance*. Their teacher, Mrs Ridler, writes:

The Reception children really enjoy being part of the school's values work, but I find they need lots of stories to help them understand what the value looks like in practice. Perseverance is a difficult concept to explain without concrete examples of how the characters demonstrate the value in a range of contexts. Mary Seacole had a complex and eventful life so we decided to just focus on her involvement in helping the soldiers in the Crimean War. I used a very simple cursion of the story and much to the delight of my class, some Year 2 children helped by dressing up and acting out the story as I read it. There was a recurring refrain throughout the story that the children joined in with.

The Story

Narrator: Mary Seacole grew up in Jamaica helping her mother to run a hotel for men who had been soldiers. As a small girl Mary was amazed and excited by the tales of bravery and adventure that the soldiers told.

When she was older, Mary heard news about fighting taking place many miles away in a place called the Crimea. She heard that badly injured soldiers had no hospitals or nurses to look after them. Mary decided to travel all the way from Jamaica to the War Office in London to ask the British Army to send her to the Crimea as a nurse.
But the Army said "No thank you".
So did Mary Seacole give up?

Children: *No, Mary Seacole persevered.*

Narrator: Mary Seacole used her own money to pay for a ticket on a boat to take her to the Crimea. When she arrived she went to the hosipital and offered to help.

Teacher: Did Mary Seacole give up?
Children: No, Mary Seacole persevered!

But the nurses said "No thank you".
So did Mary Seacole give up?

Children: *No, Mary Seacole persevered.*

She decided to set up her own hotel for injured soldiers so they had a safe and comfortable place to get better. Mary collected driftwood, packing cases and iron sheets, whatever she could find and began to build the hotel herself. Other people came to help her. When the hotel was finished, Mary served refreshments and sold the soldiers things that they needed like soap, clothes and combs. She looked after their cuts and bruises and gave them medicine and ointment, but Mary knew that where the fighting was happening many soldiers were lying injured on the battlefield and couldn't move. I must go to them and help them she thought.

But Mary's friends said "No, it is too dangerous.
So did Mary Seacole give up?

Children: *No, Mary Seacole persevered.*

Narrator: When Mary went to the injured soldiers, she wore bright clothes with red ribbons in her bonnet so that the soldiers could recognise her and see her coming. She washed their wounds, gave them medicines, bandaged them up and tried to make them better. Many soldiers were very, very thankful to Mary. When the war was over Mary Seacole had used all her money and all her strength. When she went back to England she was poor and ill. But the old soldiers did not forget the kindness and perseverance of Mary Seacole. They organised a big collection. Lots of people gave money to help Mary and say a big thank you for all she had done.

In the classroom, we made brightly coloured dressing up clothes available and 'built' a hospital ward with bandages, water, cotton wool and blankets for role play activities.

The children have loved learning about Mary Seacole and now have a very concrete idea about what it means to persevere even when life is difficult.

"I thank thee, O Lord our Creator, that thou has permitted me to look at the beauty in thy work of creation."

Johannes Kepler

Value: Thankfulness
A Themed Curriculum Day
Year groups - 1 and 2
Class Teacher - Mrs Shahne Vickery

We had undergone a particularly cold and snowy spell of weather and the children were really excited. Our theme in collective worship that term had been thankfulness and inspired by some ideas in a book by Margaret Cooling called *Assemblies That Count*[1], I decided to suspend the planned curriculum for the day.

We began by watching a BBC Schools programme about the seasons, which showed snowflakes and how they were formed from ice crystals. I then told the story of Johannes Kepler a famous mathematician who lived some four centuries ago. It was Kepler who first discovered the six pointed pattern that was common to all snowflakes and also realised that every snowflake was different. Kepler was a Christian and when he considered the millions of fantastically beautiful flakes that fall every time it snows, he was overwhelmed with thankfulness to God for the gift of being able to see and study this breathtaking sight.

He wrote
"I thank thee, O Lord our Creator,
that thou has permitted me to look
at the beauty in thy work of creation.
I exalt thee in the work of thy hands."

Harmony of the World – Kepler

We then all donned hats, coats and gloves and set out for a walk in nearby woods to enjoy the magic of the crisp and crunchy snow beneath our feet and the snow lined branches overhead.

When we returned to school I showed the children how to cut a snowflake shape by folding paper and cutting patterns into the folds. When our snowflakes were made we stuck them onto coloured sheets of paper. I challenged the children to find the lines of symmetry in the shapes.

After break we used Clive Sansom's poem "Snowflakes" as the stimulus and looked for rhyme and rhythm.

---

1 Assemblies That Count by Margaret Cooling, publ. Stapleford Centre, 2000

"Each star is newly forged, as faces are."

Clive Sansom

As well as introducing the children to some new vocabulary, the poem beautifully conveys the wonder and mystery of the snowflake.

Snowflakes
And did you know
That every flake of snow
That forms so high
In the grey winter sky
And falls so far
Is a bright six-pointed star?
Each crystal grows
A flower as perfect as a rose.
Lace could never make
The patterns of a flake.
No brooch
Of figured silver could approach
Its delicate craftsmanship. And think:
Each pattern is distinct.
Of all the snowflakes floating there –
The million million in the air –
None is the same. Each star

Is newly forged, as faces are,
Shaped to its own design
Like yours and mine.
And yet… each one
Melts when its flight is done;
Holds frozen loveliness
A moment, even less;
Suspends itself in time –
And passes like a rhyme.

In our music lesson later in the day the children used untuned percussion instruments to create a sound accompaniment whilst the poem was performed.

Finally we returned to the story of Kepler for our end of day class worship and reflected on his response of thankfulness to having been the very first person to discover what a snowflake was really like. I asked the children for examples of sights in creation that caused them to be thankful. We then included these in an extemporary class prayer.

Not only do the children thoroughly enjoy our RE days but they really allow us time to explore in some depth the "big questions" in our syllabus.

Value: Creativity
Curriculum Area – RE
KS1 unit - Who made the world?
KS2 unit - What is God like?
Head Teacher - Jane Leo

Jane Leo is the Headteacher and RE subject leader at Horton Voluntary Aided C of E Primary School. At least twice a year, the whole school, 47 children, comes together for an RE focus day. Jane writes:

> *Not only do the children thoroughly enjoy our RE days but they really allow us time to explore in some depth the "big questions" in our syllabus. Previously we have had days on religious festivals, special saints and most recently we spent a day in our ancient parish church, St. Mary's, finding out about how it had been used as a place of worship down the centuries. Our value for this term is Creativity and we planned our RE day around the Key Stage 1 unit Who made the world? and the Key Stage 2 unit What is God like? The aim of the day was to grow in our understanding of the nature of God as creator by studying the natural wonders of creation in our rural setting.*

It was a great privilege to be invited with the Living Values photographer, Joff Fitch, to spend part of a day at Horton School to observe and try to capture some of the learning that took place. The day began with collective worship at which Mrs Leo showed a stunning PowerPoint© presentation of some of the wonders of creation with an accompanying sound track.

When this was finished she asked the children to close their eyes and recall in their mind one of the images they had seen and to think of two or three adjectives to describe the picture. These were some of the children's suggestions: stunning, powerful, peaceful, dramatic, awesome, colourful, scary. Mrs Leo then asked a child to read the following Bible passage.

"God's eternal power and character cannot be seen. But from the beginning of creation God has shown what these are like by all he has made."

Romans 1:20

Christians believe that it is possible to understand more about God as Creator by observing carefully the things he has made.

She explained that when we look carefully at great pieces of art or wonderful poetry or listen to a great piece of music, we can often learn something about the person who created it. Christians believe that it is possible to understand more about God as Creator by observing carefully the things he has made. Mrs Leo asked the children to look again at the list of their words that she had written on the whiteboard and asked them to consider how many of these words might also be used to describe God. She concluded with a prayer of thanksgiving for the riches and variety of the world around us.

The school was then divided into key stage groups. We joined the younger children who were invited by their teacher to take cameras out into the school grounds and photograph images in creation that they believed helped them to think about God as a Creator. When they returned and uploaded their pictures, these were some of the children's comments.

Miles "My picture of a tiny spider showed me that God loves everything that he has made even though some people don't like spiders."

Livvy "I photographed a snail track which showed me that God created snails to know where they have been."

Charlie "I took what I could see through the school gate – I saw all my friends and that God had made them all different."

Poppy "I photographed some plants in our garden to show that God is in everything that grows."

The teacher wanted the children to explore the justice issues resulting from the dilemma faced by the government.

Value: Justice
Curriculum Area – Geography
Year Group - 5

The context for the following lessons was a unit of work on the rainforest in a Year 5 class. The school was also several weeks into a focus on the value Justice.

The class had studied the geographical features of the rainforest, its biodiversity and ecological importance as well as the economic realities of the indigenous population.

The teacher now wanted the children to explore the justice issues resulting from the dilemma faced by the government who had received a request for permission to clear a substantial area of the forest.

It was decided to use the Mantle of the Expert strategy to encourage the children to consider what a 'just' solution would be for the wildlife and plant life as well as dealing compassionately with the very poor people who needed to cultivate the land to make a living.

The teacher explained that the government minister would be holding a public meeting to which everyone in the community with a vested interest would be invited.

Half the class was given the task of putting forward the environmental case and the belief that there should be absolutely no more deforestation. The other half were charged with presenting a reasoned argument for controlled clearing of land for economic purposes.

The class was given the rest of the lesson in the IT suite to research their cases. Each group were then asked to elect three people to present the different aspects of each case. It was suggested that these people sit on an expert panel and the rest of the class in the public gallery.

Finally, the teacher arranged the classroom to simulate a public hall and welcomed the children in his role as the government official. He then ran the session as a formal public meeting allowing each group to make their case, drawing on expert witnesses and local residents to give evidence. When all the arguments were heard, the teacher, in his role as government official summed up and put the options to a vote.

VALUES: THE SCHOOL ENVIRONMENT

Primary Schools are vibrant, colourful and interactive learning environments where those things that are important in the life of the community are celebrated in displays and installations in and around the building.

At St. Andrew's Voluntary Aided Church of England Primary School in Chedworth the staff team pays great attention to giving their core values a high visual profile.

In this chapter Tina Buck, Headteacher and Angharad Fitch, RE Co-ordinator, take us on a tour around their school.

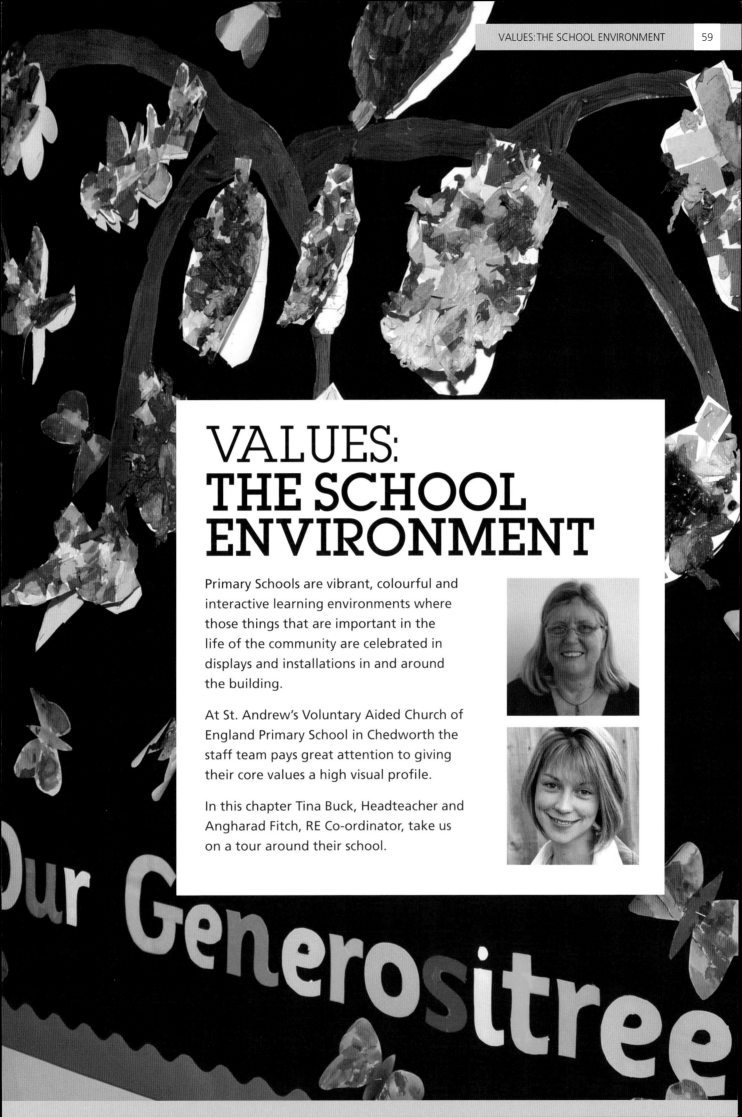

As soon as visitors enter our school we want them to be made aware of the particular values that are important to us as a community.

Mindful that there is a wide variety of learning styles represented in every class and many children are visual learners we, at St. Andrew's Primary School, ensure that our displays are bold, well-designed and interactive.

As soon as visitors enter our school we want them to be made aware of the particular values that are special to us as a community. We have recently been inspired by a display at Cam Hopton Primary School that shows each value as a flower. The children there have done some research and discovered that each of the different values has a flower associated with it. We have decided to base our new entrance display on this excellent idea. Our value for this term is *Generosity,* so we will *plant* gladioli!

In the shared area between the classrooms there is always a reflection station that is used by everyone – children, staff, parents and governors – to take time to think about and pray for the people and events that are most important to us. We often use the *Pause to Reflect on Values*[1] resource as our inspiration

for these stations. The example shown on the page opposite is based on the story that Jesus told about a party to which everyone is invited. It helps us reflect on how inclusive we are, or are not, both as individuals and as a school.

As children make their way to the hall for collective worship there is a reminder of the particular aspect of the value which is the theme for the week. *See opposite.*

Last term when we focused on the value *Creativity* we discovered that people in some countries make colourful crosses from discarded items. This is not only done out of necessity, because the people are very poor, but also because it reminds them that Jesus was rejected by his followers and crucified on a cross at Golgotha – the rubbish tip outside the city walls of Jerusalem. Our cross as we approach the hall is a visual representation of this. *See opposite.*

1 Pause to Reflect on Values, published by Jumping Fish Ltd 2010

This is our version of The Big Party, based on Jesus' teaching in the Parable of The Great Feast (Luke 14)

The Big Party

Value	Generosity
Resources	Party paraphernalia, eg party hats, plates and cups, party cloth, balloons, imitation party cake with candles, gift-wrapped parcels (one with posting slot).
Words	

> Jesus told a story about deciding who to invite to a party. The story helped people to understand that God invites everyone to be His friend, not only rich, important and famous people.
>
> Inviting someone to join in with you can make them feel special and included. How could you do this? Think of a person you would like to invite and secretly write their name on one of the small invitation cards and post it in the slot in this gift box. This will help you to remember to include that person in many ways.

Prepare the children by:
- Sharing a story about parties.
- Talking about different types of parties, eg family occasions, birthday parties, Christmas parties, New Year parties, house warmings etc.
- Talking to children about what they enjoy about parties.
- Showing a party invitation and asking who they might invite if they were organising the party (it is not always possible to invite everyone in the class).
- Reading 'The Big Party' from the Lion Storyteller Bible (by Bob Hartman) and asking what the children think about this story.

Review with the children by:
- Asking the children to describe how they felt when they included someone new in an activity.
- Asking the children to talk about how they themselves have felt when they've been left out of an activity they would have liked to be a part of.

The reverse side of The Big Party taken from Pause to Reflect on Values © Jumping Fish Ltd

Each week our lunchtime supervisors nominate a particular child who has demonstrated the value in an outstanding way.

Our lunchtime supervisors are very involved in promoting positive behaviour in the playground and reinforcing the current value in their informal and incidental conversations with the children. Each week they nominate a particular child who has demonstrated the value in an outstanding way. The Courtesy Cup is presented to that pupil during our celebration worship on a Friday. Indira received the Courtesy Cup for showing generosity to others in the dining hall by helping the younger children with their lunch.

The child takes the cup home for the weekend and returns it on Monday to sit on the worship table until the following Friday.

Children are also invited to nominate other members of the school community that they have witnessed living out our special value during the week. They do this by writing names on the laminated *value sheets* posted around the school. This very simple activity has really helped children to understand what the value means in practice. During our celebration worship, children are invited to come to the front and encourage us all by talking about the positive behaviour that they have seen and heard around the school.

Throughout the term we will encourage children and teachers to look out for both local and national newspaper reports of real life examples of people demonstrating the value *Generosity* in the public domain. This helps us all to appreciate that there is a lot of good news in the world and that there are many people trying to make the world a better place.

In each classroom there is a display or reflection activity which interprets the value in a way that is appropriate to the year group. This term my class created a GenerosiTree. Everyone invented and made an fantastical, exotic fruit to hang on the tree. When the fruit was flipped over, the children had written an example of what life might be like in the class if we were all generous to each other. *(See page 59 for picture of display.)*

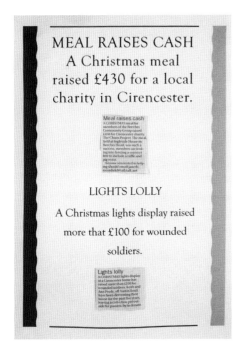

Some of the pledges to lend a hand have been very ingenious and have really encouraged children to think about different types of generosity.

In another class they have been thinking about what it means to give time generously. Children make *15 minute pledges* to lend a hand to family or friends. The pledge is then signed by both parties and the hands on the *Generosity Clock* are moved on a quarter of an hour. Each time a twelve hour cycle is completed the whole class has a fun treat! Some of the pledges have been very ingenious and really encouraged children to think about different types of generosity, like being patient when showing younger children how to play complicated games, sharing their own stationery with others or giving generously from their pocket money towards the work of our school charity.

Not all the children at St. Andrews live in the village. Some parents bring children to the school because of its particular ethos. It is therefore important to establish a sense of community and belonging from the beginning of each year. In September I ask every child in my class to choose from a collection of pebbles. Each pebble is a different colour and shape and has unique markings. The children do a painting of their pebble and write a short paragraph to describe it, then this text is attached to the painting. The pictures are laid out randomly on the floor and then the children work in pairs to try to match the pebble to the appropriate painting and description. I then talk to the children about the fact that just as the pebbles are all different, each of us is unique. The pebbles are then placed in a bowl of water (the water symbolising God's love surrounding and uniting us as a community). At the start of each class act of worship we light three floating candles on the surface of the water that remind us of God as Trinity, Father, Son and Holy Spirit. We also say the Generosity Collect, which collects together the worship scenes developed for this value in *Values for Life*. The collect is displayed in all the classrooms throughout the term.

The Generosity Collect[1]
Generous God
You have given us so much in our lives that is good.
Help us to give of our time freely
          our talents humbly
          and our energy enthusiastically
to all with whom we share our lives. Amen.

1 A pack of illustrated, photocopiable laminated A3 posters displaying a collect for each of the 18 values in *Values for Life*, publication 2012.

Get Well Prayer Box

Every new child is invited to add their painted pebble to create a visual reminder that each member of our school community is unique and included.

Class 3 has responsibility for caring for part of our spiritual garden. They have been thinking about the words of Jesus in the Gospel of Matthew,

"Your giving should be done in secret. Your Father will see what is done in secret, and he will reward you." (Matthew 6.4)

Each spring every child is invited to plant a tiny seed, as a symbol of a secret promise that they make before God to show generosity to someone in need. When the flowers bloom the children will be reminded that even the smallest act of kindness can grow into something beautiful.

For the last two years our school has taken part in Experience Easter[1]. This is one of four 'Experience Journeys' that are often set up in the local church by its members. Each journey comprises a series of interactive stations, which tell the stories behind the major Christian festivals in creative, child-friendly ways. As we were thinking about *Generosity* this term

I decided to set up the Servant King station in class. This tells the story of Jesus taking the towel and washing the disciples' feet. At the end, the children are invited to dip their fingers in the water and make a sign of the cross on each palm as they think of ways to serve others in a special way during the Easter festival.

Each week the Get Well cards made by pupils and placed in the prayer box, are taken to the local parish church and used by the congregation to pray for people in the school community who are poorly.

We are a small school and it takes precious time and energy for staff to think of lots of creative ways to engage children visually. However, we have found that just talking about our values is not enough. Learning is always multi-sensory and the school environment offers so many opportunities to make the values thought provoking, relevant, challenging and fun!

VALUES:
THE OUTDOOR
SPACE

Martin Fry is the Headteacher of Horsley
Church of England Primary School. This
popular, 4 class school is wedged between
the graveyard for the parish church on
one side and the village high street on
the other. In this chapter Martin describes
how his highly innovative use of outdoor
space has created an inspirational working
environment for the school. Rob Stephens,
the Buildings and Admissions Adviser for the
Diocese of Gloucester, goes on to explain
how a groundbreaking project to re-order
the local church has provided additional,
much needed, multi-functional space for
Horsley School.

Two of the values at Horsley C of E Primary School that are fundamental to our ethos are 'creativity' and 'community'.

Two of the values at Horsley C of E Primary School that are fundamental to our ethos are *Creativity* and *Community.* We believe that these values are key to ensuring that the broadest opportunities are offered to each child and that our church school is at the very heart of the local community.

Having utilised every square centimetre of space within our tiny Victorian building, including installing a mezzanine floor to make an extra classroom, it became increasingly clear that we needed to think creatively about our outdoor areas.

We wanted children to share the ownership of the redesigned outdoor environment with the school staff and architects. In order to afford each child access to this process we used a variety of approaches to consultation. Children drew pictures, designed plans, constructed models and formulated questionnaires to make sure everyone had a voice and an input into the planning process. These are some of the children's hopes and dreams:

- A safe area for ball games
- A wild space for nature activities
- A quiet corner for reading and reflection
- A stage for performances
- A covered area for worship and teaching
- A story-telling seat
- An outdoor exhibition area for art installations
- A climbing and fitness area
- An area suitable for dance and gymnastics
- A growing garden in addition to the orchard
- An outdoor learning area for the Reception class

Parents were involved through a questionnaire and we then tapped into their expertise in the planning stage. The results of the consultation process were somewhat daunting especially as the school field and play area is steeply sloped and can only be accessed by leaving the school premises and walking a few metres along the High Street pavement!

The performance arts have a high profile at Horsley School.

We envisaged our dream school as a kind of jigsaw and we focused on the different elements piece by piece. Our first stage was developing the 'L' shaped playground and sloped grass area. At the highest point we created an outdoor classroom and worship space. This location is very peaceful and is particularly suitable for spiritual activities, as the view of the surrounding countryside is magnificent. This pavilion type structure is very versatile and brilliant for exhibiting children's artwork. The installations often serve as inspirational foci for our worship.

Dropping down the slope, the grassy area which was used previously for ball games saw small changes that widened opportunities for children at break and lesson time: a small orchard with apple trees, a chess board, a long willow tunnel to the outside classroom and garden plots for flowers, fruit and vegetables.

Below this at two levels we introduced three tarmaced areas, one for small ball games, one with climbing apparatus and the other for netball or football - 3 spaces for different activities that cater for all.

With creativity being one of our key values, the performance arts have a high profile at Horsley. A covered stage was essential. The space that was designed is multi-functional and has been used for evening play performances including The Tempest, A Midsummer Night's Dream and various musical recitals. The space is also used by our musicians at tea parties and other social functions, for charity cake sales run by the children and as a venue for Harvest lunch. It also acts as another play area at lunchtimes. Once again the children were fully engaged in the design including the mural on the wall depicting the local area.

As in all good projects, these areas continue to develop and the latest addition is a story-telling chair. Originally designed to be made in wood, the children had concerns that it may not be as durable as one made from stone. A local mason was therefore commissioned to create a seat from the children's design of a tree with creatures. As well as for sitting in to tell stories, this chair is used for quiet reflection, reading or as a Friendship Bench.

An agreement with the PCC and the Diocese supported our idea of building a decking area, accessible from the classroom.

Next we turned our attention to the need for an outside area for the Reception class.

This posed particularly unusual challenges. We did have the play areas with all the requirements for a foundation stage curriculum but up the road! Back at school the only direction possible for extension was out into the graveyard. An agreement with the PCC and the Diocese supported our idea of building a decking area accessible from the classroom, thereby avoiding any disturbance to ancient graves. Once again the aim was to make the space work in many ways. The secure decking area built on different levels provides opportunities for varied activities: a long flat run for bikes, skittles or running games doubles up as a place for parents to wait when collecting their children. Above this, the higher level areas are ideal for construction, painting, puppet theatre, small games or telling stories.

The children's desire for an area for gymnastics, dance and celebrating the Arts caused us to really think out of the box. A beautiful and spacious parish church stands adjacent to our school. As with many churches, its use was limited for the most part to an hour or so on a Sunday. The PCC had kindly allowed the school to use the end of the nave for worship and performances for a few years but the possibilities of developing *this special place* for *all* was my dream. It seemed to me a travesty that the need of the school for a hall was so great and yet the church building on our doorstep was lying cold and empty so much of the time. With full backing from the Governors and Diocesan Buildings Adviser, we approached the PCC with some radical ideas that would involve a substantial re-ordering of the church building. This was the beginning of a long, at times exasperating but exciting journey that would inspire others in the future.

It was necessary to consider all options in order to provide a large multi-functional space for their creative and spiritual activities.

Robert Stephens, Schools Buildings and Admissions Adviser for the Gloucester Diocese takes up the story.

It was clear that for Horsley Primary to grow and thrive as a Church school, seeking to be at the heart of the community that it serves and living out its Christian values, it was necessary to consider all options in order to provide a large multi-functional space for their creative and spiritual activities.

At this time churches in our diocese are being encouraged to make the most of their buildings in order to offer maximum flexibility for both church and community. The parish therefore, as well as the school, was keen to explore possibilities for making the most of this church building which stands at the centre of the village.

Due to the very constrained site at Horsley, the school had already been making use of the church building to a limited degree for worship and some performance work. The presence of a large number of pews however, as well as the poor condition of the floor and inadequate heating, meant that the space was far from ideal! A long process of collaboration began with members of the Parochial Church Council who were naturally concerned that the church should retain the character of a place of worship. This enterprise was such a complex undertaking because the priorities of church, school and community were often very different. However, a design was finally agreed and local architects, engineers and builders were engaged to take the project forward. In many ways this venture was a ground breaking one for our diocese and we have all learned a great deal from the challenges that have been met and overcome. The result is really spectacular and has realised everyone's hopes and dreams. The materials that have been used and the sensitivity of the re-ordering have enabled the church to retain its integrity and beauty as a place of worship whilst providing a safe, warm multi-functional space for the school and village community.

Before, hard floors, splinters, and plain cold walls. Now, this church has been renovated into a splendid, beautiful, peaceful place.

By Ellie Jones-Jobst Age 11

The pews are now gone and replaced by easily stackable chairs discreetly housed in specially designed cupboards, made by reusing the old floor boards, which extend the full length of the walls. Energy efficient heating has been installed under a new floor. The floor boards have also been used for the cupboards in a purpose-built kitchen and to construct a toilet block near the entrance. A new lighting scheme, which includes stage lights mounted on the old wooden beams, enables a range of lighting effects to be created.

In the churchyard the path linking the church to the school has been resurfaced, and is illuminated at night by a series of lights. A small car park has been made within the existing boundary wall.

The official opening was a multi-sensory expression of the schools values of community and creativity. It brought together school, church, village and diocese in a great service of celebration led by the Bishop of Gloucester.

Now that the work is successfully completed and Horsley Parish Church is used almost continually seven days a week, I have the opportunity to reflect on what we have learned. Listed are some essential requirements that I believe should be considered before embarking on a project of this nature:

- A clear vision that is shared by the diocese, school and local church for the building

- A clear financial plan and effective fundraising team

- Clarity regarding the legal aspects of the project eg. workable lease agreement

- Consultation with the local community

- An understanding of the range of uses intended for the building

- An appreciation of the constraints and sensitivities, as well as the opportunities, of using a place of worship for school and community activities.

Perhaps the impact of the building is best summed up by Ellie, aged 11, in her words above.

VALUES: HOME/SCHOOL LINKS

Debbie Helme teaches at St. Mary's Voluntary Aided Church of England School in Tetbury where she co-ordinates R.E. When some of the parents at St. Mary's expressed an interest to know more about the school's values in order that they could talk about them and apply them with their children at home, Debbie agreed to write a leaflet for each value to provide information, discussion starters, quizzes and short stories for families to share. A new publication, 'At Home with Values', to include leaflets for all 18 values is planned.

We began by distributing posters of our current value around the school.

For a while at St. Mary's we have been considering ways of enhancing the profile of the 'value for life' in our school and wider community.

Initially we began by distributing posters of our current value around the school so that the whole school community from the children through to the dinner ladies and visitors would know which value we were focussing on and be able to be involved with our learning.

Then we extended this idea into the outdoor space. We used the same style of poster and illustration out in the playground, but we developed this further by inviting the children to use their senses to contemplate aspects of the value. For example, for *Peace* we thought about sounds and listening and for *Compassion* we thought about feelings and touch.

This immediately attracted the attention of some of the parents who became aware of the values being taught at school. We began to include brief details about our value in our weekly newsletter and some parents then requested further information.

Encouraged by this response we invited parents to come to a parent/teacher working group. A number of requests and ideas were suggested. The parents were keen to know how the individual values were introduced and explained to the children within school. They were generally keen to encourage conversation and discussion about the value at home but some felt they needed support and ideas to initiate such debate.

One parent requested Biblical references and additional information specifically for adults so they could learn more about the value themselves. Another parent wondered if there were creative ways that the whole family could consider and learn together about the value. Others asked for some suggestions of children's books that would stimulate discussion about values.

Buoyed up by all the enthusiasm, we decided to put together easily photocopiable leaflets to be made available to parents on request[1]. We tried to include as many of the parent's ideas as possible and the following examples are based on our first attempts.

1 *At Home With Values* is a set of photocopiable activity sheets to support families who want to explore the value together, publication 2012.

AT HOME WITH VALUES

Dear Parents, This term we will be focussing on the value of **PERSEVERANCE**. If you would like to explore this value further at home we hope that you will find this leaflet helpful.

TALK ABOUT... PERSEVERANCE

As a family, discuss things that each of you can do now that you have needed perseverance to learn.

Parents, tell your child about the times that you remember them learning to walk or dress themselves.

What activities did they find easy/hard? Can you think of a time when they felt like giving up?

What helped them to persevere? What made things worse? Talk about times that you have had to persevere. What helps you keep going?

VALUE CHALLENGE CUP

Look on the Value Board on our school entrance hall to find out last term's winners.

Mosaics are one of the oldest ways to make art. People have been arranging tiny coloured pieces of glass or pottery for thousands of years to create beautiful designs. This term's Value Challenge is to make a mosaic picture (no bigger than A3 – 29x42cm) using small pieces of coloured paper. The subject of your mosaic is up to you. It could be a pattern or a picture.

All the pictures submitted will be displayed in our school gallery.

A BIBLE STORY ABOUT... PERSEVERANCE

The Lost Sheep (Luke 15: 3-7)

Jesus once told his followers a story.

The shepherd knew each one of his sheep. They were all important and every one was precious. He led them out of the sheep pen and into the hills to find greenest and juiciest grass. Sometimes it was hard to find good pasture in the dry, rocky countryside, but he persevered because he cared.

At the end of the day he brought them back to the pen and counted them safely in. But one evening he discovered that one of his precious sheep was missing. The shepherd counted them again and again until he was sure; one of his sheep was lost!

That night the shepherd went out onto the dark hills. He searched and searched, getting colder and colder, but never once did he think of giving up. Eventually, far out into the night, he heard the faintest, weakest bleat. Listening very carefully, he followed the sound until, there it was – his lost sheep tangled up and trapped in a huge thorny bush. He carried it home until it was back once again with all the other sheep, safe and sound.

God is like that shepherd, Jesus said. His love is so great that he never gives up on anyone.

p	e	r	s	e	v	e	r	a	n	c	e
s	d	e	p	p	a	r	t	d	e	g	d
u	e	d	o	g	g	o	h	a	o	n	d
o	v	e	r	j	o	y	e	d	u	r	h
l	e	d	r	t	o	a	h	o	e	t	e
c	l	d	e	s	t	h	s	h	n	a	e
e	l	o	y	h	a	a	p	g	v	t	e
r	e	n	h	r	c	e	r	s	s	s	s
p	r	f	d	e	h	r	m	h	c	u	t
l	o	s	t	s	e	r	a	e	s	l	o
m	l	s	s	l	n	g	b	e	f	a	s
d	e	l	g	n	a	t	j	p	s	t	l

god	missing	relieved	shepherd
hard	overjoyed	safe	sound
jesus	perseverance	searched	tangled
lost	precious	sheep	trapped

Stories in fiction about Perseverance
- Lost & Found by Oliver Jeffers, Harper Collins
- Who are you stripy horse? by Jim Helmore, Egmont
- Out of the Ashes by Michael Morurgo, MacMillan

FASCINATING FACTS ABOUT PERSEVERANCE... IN NATURE

A mole can dig a tunnel 100m long in one night.

An arctic tern, a bird that lives mainly in North America, flies to the Antarctic each year – a journey of 40,000 km.

A tortoise walks and runs slowly (2 km/hour) but can keep going for long periods of time without resting.

A TRUE TALE ABOUT... PERSEVERANCE

Prince George had always been shy. His father was the King of England.

The young prince developed a stammer which meant he could not speak for very long without struggling to say the words he wanted to say. His elder brother, Edward, was very different. He was confident and loved to be the centre of attention. Because he was the eldest it was Edward who would one day become king when their father died.

And that is what happened. But soon after the coronation King Edward announced that he was going to abdicate – to give up being king. His younger brother would now become king in his place. George was horrified! He felt sick with fright. Now he who would be expected to deliver speeches and give radio broadcasts to millions! How would he be able to do this with his dreadful stammer? But George knew that it was his duty to serve his country. He knew that he must overcome his fears and do his very best. He employed an Australian speech therapist to help him and with perseverance and great courage George was able to face the challenges ahead.

When war was declared in 1939 King George gave a famous speech. He comforted and encouraged his people and won everyone's respect because they knew how brave he was being.

The story of King George VI has inspired the film The King's Speech starring Colin Firth. The film won many awards and millions of people have watched it. Why do you think the story has inspired so many?

> *If at first you don't succeed, try, try and try again…*
> *Robert Burns*

FAMILY CHALLENGE

This game requires bravery on the part of both adults and children!

Everyone has to think of something they find quite easy that another member of the family may find difficult, eg. a child could challenge a parent to match their time in achieving a level in a game on a Wii, DS, Xbox or Playstation game. An adult could challenge a child to reciting one of the times tables in a minute or tackling the washing up after Sunday lunch etc.

Encourage everyone to keep going even when they find the going tough. What helps them to keep trying? For example encouragement, support and help.

Talk about the ways your family members can support each other. Can you all ask for help when you need it?

THE PERSEVERANCE LADDER

Can members of your family climb up the Perseverance Ladder by finding ways to persevere with boring, difficult or challenging tasks? Write in the gaps between the rungs the tasks you set yourselves and climb the ladder!

AT HOME WITH VALUES

Dear Parents, This term we will be focussing on the value of **PEACE**. If you would like to explore this value further at home we hope that you will find this leaflet helpful.

TALK ABOUT...PEACE

There are a number of aspects of Peace that we shall be considering as a school this year. We will be thinking about peaceful places, feeling at peace with oneself, being a peacemaker in times of argument and conflict and peace in the world. We shall also be exploring what the Bible meant when it describes Jesus as 'The Prince of Peace' (Isaiah 9:6).

As a family you may want to talk about:

- Where each of you go when you want to be peaceful and quiet

- How you respond if people around you are arguing

- Ways that you can help to bring peace and reconciliation

- What or who helps to bring you peace when you feel upset or worried inside?

- You can talk about people in the news who are trying to bring peace locally, nationally or globally.

> What can you do to promote world peace? Go home and love your family.
> *Mother Teresa*

Other stories from the Bible about Peace
(Use a good Children's Bible - ask at school for recommended versions)
- The message of Isaiah - Isaiah 2,3, 11
- Mary, Martha and Lazarus - Luke 10 Psalm 23

Other stories in fiction about Peace
- Peace at Last by Jill Murphy, MacMillan
- The Seeds of Peace by Laura Berkeley, Barfoot
- The War Game by Michael Foreman, Puffin

PSALM 23 Good News Translation (GNT)

The Lord is my shepherd;
1 have everything I need.
2 He lets me rest in fields of green grass
and leads me to quiet pools of fresh water.
3 He gives me new strength.
He guides me in the right paths,
as he has promised.
4 Even if I go through the deepest darkness,
I will not be afraid, Lord,
for you are with me.
Your shepherd's rod and staff protect me.

5 You prepare a banquet for me,
where all my enemies can see me;
you welcome me as an honoured guest
and fill my cup to the brim.
6 I know that your goodness and love will be with me all my life;
and your house will be my home as long as I live.

WORD GRID

Fit the words from Psalm 23 into the grid

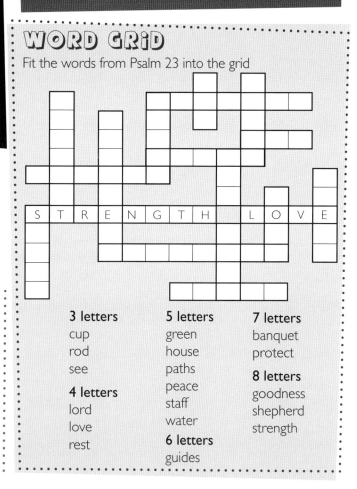

3 letters	5 letters	7 letters
cup	green	banquet
rod	house	protect
see	paths	
	peace	**8 letters**
4 letters	staff	goodness
lord	water	shepherd
love		strength
rest	**6 letters**	
	guides	

FAMILY CHALLENGE

Invite all the family into the garden, go to the park or on a wet day stay in one room. Everyone will need a pen and paper and then have 2 minutes to write down or draw anything they can hear. No one is allowed to deliberately make noise themselves. The winner will be the person who heard the most sounds.

You could repeat this game using different senses, for example how many textures can you feel or colours can you see? Or focus on how many different bird songs you can hear? Can you try and identify them?

VALUE CHALLENGE CUP

Think of scenes that make you feel peaceful or calm. It maybe unusual cloud formations, still water or flowers. It may be a particular person. Discuss different ideas as a family.

Together go on a photo shoot. Let everyone have a turn taking a photographs. Select and mount the photograph you all think makes you feel most 'peaceful'.

We will display all the photographs in the entrance hall at school anonymously. There will be an opportunity for all the children to vote for their favourite 'peaceful' scene and the photo with the most votes will be this term's cup winner.

Please provide photos with name and class on the back and entries must be handed in by the end of term.

A FAMOUS DOVE

This image is a drawing by Pablo Picasso. He once explained that his father had taught him to paint doves, adding 'I stand for life against death; I stand for peace against war'.

A PRAYER FOR PEACE

Write a family prayer for peace in this dove shape.

VALUES: CHURCH/ SCHOOL LINKS

Catherine Coster is an ordained minister in the Church of England, a part-time RE Consultant and a Foundation Governor at Horton Voluntary Aided Church of England Primary School. Whilst Schools Adviser in the Bristol Diocese, Catherine co-wrote Values for Life. In this chapter she outlines some of the practical ways that Values Education can be a shared focus in the church/school partnership.

Through the Open the Book scheme teams of people use the Lion Storyteller Bible by Bob Hartman to make stories come alive for the pupils.

Following a programme of values education will automatically initiate a process of moral and spiritual exploration by all involved in the life of the school. In my experience churches have been welcomed as partners in discerning how values may be made more explicit in all the activities of the community.

Some of the examples of good practice that are included in this chapter are taken from Horton Primary School where I serve as a Foundation Governor. Others I observed whilst working as a diocesan schools adviser.

Worship

Some parishes, like my own, organise family friendly worship either in the school or in the church building. Children are able to sing the same songs that they sing at school and play a part in organising the worship. It is all the more helpful if services are themed around the particular value that a school is exploring.

Open the Book

Through the *Open the Book*[1] scheme teams of people use the Lion Storyteller Bible by Bob Hartman to make stories come alive for the pupils. As the stories of the faith are told and retold pupils can talk about and reflect on how they might shape their own behaviour and that of others. We are able to use the Bible stories in *Open the Book* to support the particular value in focus and relate this value to the children's own lives.

The Experience Journeys

Experience Easter was launched 4 years ago and is now offered to local schools by churches and cathedrals in every corner of the UK and beyond. Experience Christmas, Pentecost and Harvest have followed and now Experience Easter Outside helps churches make use of their outdoor spaces. The journeys are designed to be an interactive and multi-sensory way to bring the stories behind the Christian Festivals alive for children. Experience Harvest is particularly pertinent to Christian values as each station in the journey has as it's theme one of the Fruits of The Spirit.

1 Open the Book - www.openthebook.net

At St. Paul's Primary, Salisbury a member of the local parish church used her skills as a garden designer to create a beautiful space that is enjoyed for many different functions.

Creating a Visual Expression of the Values

In SIAS Inspection reports schools are often asked to strengthen their identity as a Church of England establishment by giving a higher profile to their Christian foundation both inside and outside the buildings. Church members can support busy teachers by offering to work collaboratively with children on mosaics, banners, reflective areas and other creative installations that illustrate and reinforce the values of the school.

Care for the school buildings and grounds

Many churches and schools are now working together on creating environments in outdoor spaces where children can find time for peaceful reflection and spiritual development. At St. Mary's C of E Primary School in Pulborough, church members have worked closely with the children and staff to create a garden in which all the plants have an association with Mary. At St. Paul's Primary, Salisbury a member of the local parish church used her skills as a garden designer to create a beautiful space that is enjoyed for many different functions.

Visitors from the Church

Church members can share their Christian perspective on many issues across various curriculum areas and particularly in RE. I was recently asked to visit a local school to talk about my role as a clergy person but this soon developed into a discussion about the value of service in the community.

Values in Action

Foundation Governors are often very active in their role linking the communities of church and school together. In one school that I know a governor assists the pupils to articulate what particular values might look like in practice. These ideas are then recorded in various ways such as a class book/photographic display, articles for newsletters and items on the website. Another governor searches through the local newspapers and current affairs websites for stories of values in action. These are then used as illustrative examples in Key Stage 2 worship.

Many church members run lunch-time and after school clubs for children in their local schools.

After School Clubs

Many church members run lunch-time and after school clubs for children in their local schools. At Horton School the Making a Difference (MAD) Club has the specific remit of raising awareness of injustice and actively making a difference. Older children find real ways to respond to perceived injustices either by taking some direct initiative themselves or by contacting organisations, their MP or others to draw attention to the situation of those in need. Pupils could:

- Create improvised drama to illustrate injustices
- Write letters
- Design posters
- Send emails
- Set up twitters
- Create a presentation for the church and/or school
- Take direct action at a local level.

Overseas Links

Schools are actively encouraged to form partnerships with other schools overseas through which children have the opportunity to experience different cultures. Many parish churches have links with other worshipping communities in different parts of the world. By participating in these church links the school can benefit in ways that wouldn't otherwise be possible.

Links with the PCC

The values work of the school can be explored and reported on at Parochial Church Council (PCC) meetings. The Headteacher from the Meadow Community School at Bitton, attends PCC meetings where the vision and values of the school are shared with church members. Not only do the members feel more informed of the priorities of the school, but the school's values have also challenged them to think more deeply about the place of Christian values in the life of the local and wider church.

We set about building a community suite at Tredworth Junior School that could be a 'one stop shop' in terms of offering a wide range of advice, support and training.

The Tredworth Family Learning Trust

According to all indicators of social deprivation, Tredworth is the most challenging area in Gloucestershire in which to raise children. When Andy Darby arrived as the new head teacher of Tredworth Junior School, it was the lowest achieving school in the county.

'Many of the parents of the children in my school have had very negative experiences of education themselves and when I arrived, there was an almost complete lack of engagement with the school. I was told that the people of Tredworth had a 'poverty of aspiration', but I just refused to believe that parents do not want to see their children get on and do well. My biggest challenge was to help them to see that education was not something to rebel against or shun but was instead the key that would unlock opportunities to a better life.

In response to this problem of engagement one of the first things we did was to establish Tredworth Family Learning Trust. Through this initiative we asked parents, 'Do you want to come to school and work with your child?' and more importantly, 'What would you like to do?' Prior to my arrival adult literacy and numeracy had been offered but the take up had been very low. This time, in response to the parents suggestions we offered aerobics, pottery, art, first aid etc. Take up was and still is phenomenal.

In 2007, two church leaders, Jan and James Burn from the Kingfisher Church in Tredworth came to see me. They explained how they were already working in our community but would like to do more. Alongside them on this visit was Mark Molden from Care for the Family. To say I was inspired by them and the range of what they had to offer would be an understatement!

We set about building a community suite at Tredworth Junior School which could be a 'one stop shop' in terms of offering a wide range of advice, support and training. Through members of the Kingfisher Church, trained and resourced by Care for the Family[1] we were able to offer courses such as 21st Century Parents and Drug Proof Your Kids.

1 www.careforthefamily.org.uk

The impact of this three way school/church/university partnership has been dramatic – not least on the effect it has on the standards that our children now reach.

The Kingfisher congregation, like us at Tredworth Junior School, are doers and together we established the core values of our partnership. The school set about raising money and in October 2010 we opened a set of three meeting rooms and a state of the art kitchen. Every course we have offered has had a 100% take up. Our relationship with Kingfisher, and Care for the Family continues to go from strength to strength.

Recently, Hartpury College, which is part of the University of the West of England, has become a third partner. The college has begun to offer adult literacy and vocational courses. This time the take up has been much better. All courses are offered free of charge to anyone living in the community, whether or not they have children at our school. If facilitators and course leaders are not paid by a third party to run a workshop, then we give our building free of charge.

Several mums, who initially came along to our courses went on to train as TAs and are now employed at our school. The impact of this three way school/church/university partnership has been dramatic - not least on the effect it has on the standards that our children now reach. Essentially we achieve at least the national expectation at L4+ for children anywhere.

I am amazed that there are not more projects in which churches and schools work together in communities. Many of our values are the same and most importantly we are all working for the good of the communities we serve.

We know that by utilising the power and expertise of the local church, the university as education provider and Care for the Family to support pastoral needs, we have actually changed lives and gradually those lives are changing Tredworth.

Tredworth Junior is not a church school, however, my experience over the last few years has left me in no doubt of the benefits to schools entering into partnerships with local churches.

VALUES: FOCUS FOR INSPECTION

Andrew Ricketts is a former secondary school teacher and Ofsted Inspector. He now works as a full time SIAS Inspector in dioceses across the south west of England. Andrew has a particular interest in evaluating the ways in which the values of a school community are interpreted and expressed by its members. In this chapter Andrew and Shahne *(see page 47)* look at how inspectors judge the impact of a school's values by careful use of questioning and observation.

The Statutory Inspection of Anglican Schools (SIAS) was introduced in September 2005 as part of Section 48 of the 2005 Education Act. Since then the SIAS framework has developed significantly so that it reflects the considerable progress that Church of England schools continue to make in developing a distinct Christian ethos. The SIAS self-evaluation process has itself played a major part in helping church schools to understand how their Christian character can make a difference to the lives of those in the school community. Nowhere has this had more impact than in the place that Christian values have at the heart of a church school's mission.

SIAS now places a far greater emphasis on the impact that Christian values make to the learning and personal development of the children. This is clearly reflected in the National Society's grade descriptors, guidance that schools and inspectors use to evaluate performance as a church school. Inspectors will consider the following, in making their judgements:

- The extent to which Christian values impact on all learners and enable them to flourish as individuals

- The extent to which Christian values consistently encourage, nourish and challenge the spiritual, moral, social and cultural development of all learners throughout the curriculum

- The extent to which Christian values motivate relationships between all members of the school community

- The extent to which Christian values are shared and celebrated through the worshipping life of the school

- The clarity of the school leaders and governors in their understanding that Christian values are central to every aspect of school life

For several years now schools have been actively engaged in developing an understanding of how to place values, which in church schools are specifically

During an inspection in one school children were talking together about whether some values were more important than others.

Christian in nature, at the very heart of all that the school does and then to adopt appropriate and effective strategies to monitor and evaluate their impact in a robust and systematic way.

Of course there is no definitive way of achieving this. Each school is different because it is a reflection of the community that it serves. Schools that have identified a Christian ethos pertinent to their own circumstances are more likely to be able to identify where this ethos makes a difference and more accurately evaluate its effectiveness. It is these schools, which articulate a clear understanding of a Christian purpose, that do well in SIAS.

The quality of questioning by inspectors will be crucial in determining whether values are being lived out in the day to day life of the school. They will be looking for evidence of an established and common language being used by everyone in the school community to discuss and explore values.

For example during an inspection in one school children were talking together about whether some values were more important than others:
'Respect is OK but we can't always respect what people say and what they do, but you must always tell the truth and you must always be generous mustn't you?' This Year 4 child was demonstrating an ability to recognise the possibility of a 'values hierarchy' and appreciate that the context might have a bearing on the interpretation of a value.

In recent years since values have had a high profile in church schools inspectors have been working to develop particular questions which will help to reveal an accurate picture of the real relevance and impact of values.

The following pages include a selection of questions, listed under the headings identified in the *National Society Toolkit*, that inspectors have used in their conversations with school leaders, teachers, children and governors. Clearly only a few will asked in any one inspection and there will be other questions not included here that are just as pertinent.

1. The extent to which Christian Values impact on all learners and enable them to flourish as individuals.

Questions for School Leaders and Governors:

- What are the core values that underpin your school ethos, how were they identified and who was involved in selecting them?

- How explicitly do the values inform your school policies especially those concerned with children's well being such as PSHE, SRE, and behaviour?

- How do you evaluate whether your school's values have an impact on children's progress in learning and the quality of teaching?

Questions for Teachers:

- Can you point to evidence that demonstrates a positive benefit to the children in your school of values education?

- In your role as a teacher, were you part of the process to select the core values for your school?

- Do you think that there has been adequate training for staff in values education?

Questions for Children:

- How did your school decide which Christian values should become the school's core values?

- Which values do you think are the most important and why?

- How do you think learning about the values helps you to live well?

2. The extent to which Christian Values consistently encourage, nourish and challenge the spiritual, moral, social and cultural development of all learners throughout the curriculum.

Questions for School Leaders and Governors:

- To what extent do Christian values underpin the whole curriculum and how are opportunities to teach them made explicit in curriculum planning?

- To what extent have school rules been rooted in an understanding of what it means to live out Christian values in practice?

- In what ways are social and emotional learning programmes informed by Christian values?

Questions for Teachers:

- How does your planning link the school's values to the rest of the curriculum?

- Can you give examples of the ways in which you link the school's behaviour policy to the core values?

Questions for Children:

- Can you give an example of how one of your school values was important in something you learnt about in class?

- Has your work on values helped you (or your class) make an important decision?

- How do you think Christian values help everyone in your school community to live and work together well?

- Many of your school values are important to people of different religious faiths as well as people who have no religious faith. Why do you think this might be?

3. The extent to which Christian Values are shared and celebrated through the worshipping life of the school.

Questions for School Leaders and Governors:

- How does collective worship offer opportunities to celebrate real life examples of values demonstrated in school, local community and on the world stage?

- Do interactive displays, prayer corners and sacred spaces offer opportunities for the school community to engage with values in their own way?

- Is there a common understanding of how spiritual development is defined in your school and the way spiritual and moral development (values education) are linked?

Questions for Teachers:

- How far do children in your class understand that Christian values are rooted in stories from the Bible eg. Compassion/The Good Samaritan?

- Can you give examples of ways in which learning about values in collective worship is extended and developed in the classroom?

- How do you use the learning environment in your classroom to offer children opportunities to reflect on the school's values?

Questions for Children:

- In what ways do acts of worship in your school help you to understand more about Christian values?

- Do children in your school have opportunities to create and lead acts of worship to share what has been learnt about values?

- Can you take me to areas of display around the school that will help me understand more about your school values?

4. The extent to which Christian Values motivate the relationships between all members of the school community.

Questions for School Leaders and Governors:

- What opportunities exist for:
    - Parents to engage with teachers eg. curriculum evenings, parents' meetings etc.
    - Parents with other parents eg PTA, parents' forum, social events etc.
    - Children with other children in different age groups eg. buddy schemes, friendship bench, peer mediation etc.
    - Governors with teachers eg. away days, governors linked to individual classes etc.
    - Governors with parents eg. open evenings and welcome evenings for parents of new pupils.
    - Governors with church community eg. PCC, special services, parish/school social events.
    - Teachers with other teachers eg. retreat days, social events etc

- What strategies are in place in your school to support conflict resolution eg. peer mediation scheme? How are these explicitly linked by the children to values education?

- How does the school environment foster the development of 'one to one' or small group relationships eg. quiet spaces, spiritual gardens?

Questions for Teachers:

- Would you say that your school is an open and happy place in which you and your colleagues enjoy working?
If so why do you think this is, if not, why not?

- Is there an active exploration amongst adults as well as children about how the school's values underpin relationships? How is this facilitated?

Continued overleaf

What strategies are in place in your school to support conflict resolution or peer mediation schemes?

4. *Continued*

• Is there clarity amongst staff about the process to resolve misunderstandings or conflict? Can you give me an example of how this works?

Questions for Children:

• Can you give an example of how learning about one of your school values has helped you to get along better with people?

• Where do you go in school and who do you speak to if you have an argument with someone and need help to sort it out?

• Do you think there are lonely people in your school, why do you think this is?

5. The clarity of the School Leaders and Governors in their understanding that Christian Values are central to every aspect of school life.

Questions for School Leaders and Governors:

• What are the strategies used by school leaders and governors to review the impact of school values including canvassing parents, staff and church community?

• Does the school development plan support the development of Values Education and is adequate time given in meetings of the Governing Body to ensure that all governors are informed of progress?

• Is there a common language developing through which all members of the school community can articulate how Christian values affect attitudes and behaviour?

• How does the appointment process ensure that new members of staff are able to support and develop the Christian values of the school?

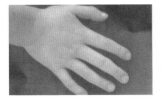   

ACKNOWLEDGEMENTS

Living Values simply would not have been possible without the huge amount of time and commitment invested in the project by Carolyn Wright, who has been responsible for collating text and images and much, much more.

I am also indebted to Stella Edwards of Sugar Ink Creative who has prepared draft after draft until this book does justice to the amazing creativity of the children and teaching staff featured within it.

And here they are...

Ashleworth Church of England Primary School, Glos

Cam Hopton Church of England Primary School, Glos

Christchurch Church of England Infants School, Downend, Bristol

Horsley Church of England Primary School

Horton Church of England Primary School

Meadow Primary School, Bitton

Nailsworth Church of England Primary School

St. Andrew's Church of England Primary School, Chedworth

St. Mary's Church of England Primary School, Tetbury

St. Mary's Church of England Primary School, Thornbury

St. Michaels High School, Crosby

St. Paul's Church of England Primary School, Gloucester

St. Paul's Church of England Primary School, Salisbury

Tredworth Junior School, Gloucester

Westbury on Severn Church of England Primary School

The schools of the Cotswold View Cluster

Tina Buck

Catherine Coster

David Crunkhurn

Andy Darby

Angharad Fitch

Martin Fry

Debbie Helme

Verity Holloway

Hayley Hutchison

Margaret James

Gary Law

Avril Muirhead

Neville Norgrove

Andrew Rickett

Robert Stephens

Foreword:

Professor Trevor Cooling

Photography:

Joff Fitch of Clements and Fitch Photography Ltd
www.clementsandfitch.co.uk

Chris Milnes Photographic Company
www.chrismilne.co.uk

Design:

Stella Edwards of Sugar Ink Creative
www.sugarink.co.uk

OTHER TITLES BY THIS AUTHOR

Values for Life *Shahne Vickery, Catherine Coster & Verity Holloway*
This flagship publication, for use in Collective Worship and across the whole curriculum, teaches 18 carefully selected values over 3 years and promotes Christian values and understanding throughout all aspects of primary school life.

Pause to Reflect on Values *Shahne Vickery, & SW region Diocesan Advisers*
Intended to support *Values for Life*, this pack gives fully worked details for creating interactive areas focusing on each of the 18 values. It is a helpful tool in promoting spiritual development throughout the whole school community.

Prayers for Life *Edited by Shahne Vickery and Carolyn Wright*
Over 100 prayers for every occasion in the life of the school community : major celebrations in the school and church year; welcoming a new headteacher; remembering a child in hospital; opening a governors' meeting ;and many more occasions.

Pause for Reflection *Shahne Vickery, & SW region Diocesan Advisers*
15 ideas for creative, interactive displays to promote spiritual development in the primary school. Each display is fully explained with instructions for assembling the reflective corner, questions to ask the children and follow up discussion ideas.

Creating a Multi-sensory Spiritual Garden in your school *Shahne Vickery*
Offers a host of practical ideas and advice for schools to create a spiritual garden. It includes photographs of school gardens throughout the UK as well as many fresh ideas for outdoor prayer and reflection activities. Each chapter focuses on one of the five senses and considers how planting, hard landscaping, art installations and wild life habitats can be used to foster children's spiritual development.

Experience Easter An imaginative approach to help children experience the Christian festival through six easy to assemble, interactive stations set up in different parts of the church. A superb opportunity to strengthen church-school links. In the series are **Experience Easter Outside**, **Experience Christmas**, **Experience Pentecost** and **Experience Harvest**.

New publications to look out for:

The Values Worship Chest Key Stage 1 collective worship ideas based on the values identified in Values for Life. A simple worship chest contains a coloured drape, reflecting the church season, and objects that reflect the theme. The children join in a simple liturgy that begins the worship, the theme is then introduced and followed by a short story and closing prayer. The pack will provide resources to support 18 values. *Publication 2012.*

At Home with Values A set of photocopiable A4 sheets to promote values beyond the school gate and support home-school links. Each term, as a new value is introduced, an activity sheet is sent home explaining the value in focus and including activities, puzzles, family challenges, discussion starters and suggested children's story books to enable the whole family to explore the value together. *Publication 2012.*

Values 'Collects' A set of prayer posters for the hall, entrance foyer or classroom walls designed to encourage children to reflect on the value in focus and live out that value in their words and actions. *Publication 2012.*

For full details and order forms see our website www.gloucester.anglican.org/resources/jfish/